MULTINATIONAL PEOPLE MANAGEMENT

A Guide for Organizations and Employees

MULTINATIONAL PEOPLE MANAGEMENT

A Guide for Organizations and Employees

by

DAVID M. NOER

A
BNA
BOOK

THE BUREAU OF NATIONAL AFFAIRS, INC., Washington, D.C.

Library of Congress Cataloging in Publication Data

Noer, David.
   Multinational people management.

   Includes index.
   1. Americans in foreign countries — Employment.
2. International business enterprises — Personnel
management. I. Title.
HF5549.5.E45N63   658.3'7'33888   75-13802
ISBN O-87179-220-6

International Standard Book Number: 0-87179-220-6
Printed in the United States of America

PREFACE

This book is written for all those who have an interest in the people aspects of multinational enterprise.

It can be of value to the employer who, knowing little of the intricacies of international people management, simply wishes to acquire a working knowledge of the subject.

It can be useful to the professional who labors daily in the trenches of multinational management and desires a basic text written by one who has also spent some time there.

It can be read by the student, or the general reader, who will find the tone not only easy to follow but of interest in understanding the multinational world that binds us all together.

And, of course, there is the expatriate, who will find his unique world explored in each chapter, with a special message at the end of each part.

Then there is the motive of the author; the desire for all involved in multinational enterprise to broaden their knowledge and increase their sensitivity to international people problems. This is necessary in order that we may develop managers with the ability to guide us through a world drawn together by the need to share energy and technology, yet pulled apart by the forces of nationalism.

TABLE OF CONTENTS

Part 3. Selection

Part 4. Orientation and Training

Part 5. Compensation Basics

Part 6. Compensation Systems

Part 7. The Future

Part 1

PEOPLE PROBLEMS

Chapter 1

INTERNATIONAL PEOPLE CRASHES

Multinational companies are involved in the movement of things across national borders. These things take the form of products and money. Multinationals also move people across borders. They encounter problems when they treat people and things the same way.

When products and money cross borders they remain basically unchanged. They are still things and, as such, do not have personalities, language problems, national biases, or culturally derived value systems. Unlike products or money, people not only experience unique problems when moved across borders but also demand individual consideration.

Corporations have sophisticated product integration systems that mesh across international borders. What do they do with the most complex and volatile of the items they move across borders? How sophisticated are they when moving people?

Many of the largest and best managed companies have no expatriate planning system at all. They simply ignore the people dimension of multinational business. In others, the method of handling international transfers is woefully inadequate for today's world. In this book we will not only outline problem areas and potential hazards in international

3

people relationships but also explore alternative solutions from both a philosophical and practical viewpoint.

These hazards relate to the real world of business and are not limited to problem people or to the so-called "hard countries." The following two examples of international people crashes will serve to put people problems into a practical perspective.

"But He Did Okay in the United States"

When it is late afternoon in Central Europe, it is morning in the Midwest, and Harvey, the worldwide sales manager for a multinational consumer goods company, was still staring at the telephone, haunted by the echoes of his first telephone call of the morning. Bill, his European sales manager, had just announced in no uncertain terms that he was coming home.

What had gone wrong? Bill was a superstar back in the United States. He had all the right ingredients for a successful sales manager; aggressive personality, total dedication to the job, willingness always to go the extra mile. When the company recognized the potential for business in Europe, there was no doubt in Harvey's mind as to who should get the job. It was Bill. Harvey would send him over there for a few years, let him shape up the local marketing organization, put local management on a sound business basis, then bring him back to the United States, where his future would be unlimited.

What had gone wrong? Harvey thought back to the telephone call.

"Got that organization turned around yet?" Harvey began. His voice was filled with optimism.

"Not exactly." Bill's voice was flat, tentative. "I'm having some problems."

"Nothing good old Bill can't handle, eh?" responded Harvey.

"Well . . . not really, these are more like personal problems."

Something really was wrong; this was not like Bill at all. He always kept personal problems inside. Harvey never could get him to open up. He had tried a few times, but it never happened.

"What's wrong—family sickness, problems with the kids?"

"No, not really . . . I . . . well, I just have to come back! Things don't seem to be working out over here."

"What! Come back?"

"Yeah, just have to. I've already booked the tickets and we leave tomorrow. Harvey, I know this will probably cost me my job, but I can't live here. It just isn't working."

When the conversation ended, Harvey studied the telephone in stunned silence. What really had gone wrong?

An analysis of the situation reveals that Bill fell victim to a severe case of a common expatriate illness—cultural shock.

He was picked to go overseas because he was the best man in the United States. This is akin to the early days of management development, when the best technical man was made the manager with the assumption that the skills would carry over. In many cases they did not, and the result was the loss of a key technical contributor and the acquisition of a bad manager.

Many companies are now utilizing more sophisticated techniques for management selection. However, a good number of managers charged with the responsibility of selecting candidates for international assignments are still laboring under the same philosophical constraints. The best in the United States is not always the best to send overseas. In fact, in Bill's case, the very qualities that made him a success in the United States contributed to his failure overseas.

Bill's aggressive, almost compulsive personality would not fit into the European business environment. His total dedication to the job had put a serious strain on his marriage. It was a strain that had nearly caused it to snap when the job and marital problems were magnified by an international assignment.

Bill's situation illustrates one of the most common causes of failure in international assignments. It is the invalid assumption that a star in the United States can transport those qualities that made him successful and operate at the same level in a different culture.

There were a number of specific reasons for Bill's failure. These were as follows:

- He had never been overseas before accepting the assignment. In fact, his family had never lived outside the Midwest. His wife, nearly widowed by Bill's total dedication to the job, was spending more and more time with her family.

- Neither he nor his wife could speak French, nor could either see the need for language training. Bill assumed that since English was spoken at Bill's office and there was a sizable English-speaking community in Brussels, it was not necessary. These assumptions were shattered the first time Bill's wife tried to buy meat from the French-speaking butcher. Bill was embarrassed when he took his first customer to dinner and could not read the menu. It was also soon apparent that Bill had to travel more and spend more time on the job in Europe. Naturally, Bill's wife could not spend time with her relatives every Sunday—a pattern she had established over the past few years.

- On the job, things just were not the same. The first day Bill called a sales meeting, threatening to fire anyone who did not meet quota. Bill soon found that you do not threaten Europeans with loss of job. The labor court system is such that it is very costly to fire people, and culturally one cannot motivate people by job threats. Bill's fear technique irreparably alienated those working for him.

- Bill, as is the case with many successful salesmen, was compulsively neat. In many European countries neatness is not as revered as in the United States. Nor, in fact, are showers or regular use of a deodorant. Bill rapidly reached the conclusion that all Europeans were slobs and smelled bad—another example of cultural values clashing.

- Many Europeans emphasize formality. Structure is very important in business. Bill liked to get to the heart of the matter, take short lunches, make rapid decisions—go, go, go. His European colleagues liked long lunches, formal discussions—slow, slow, slow.

- Bill, like many Americans, was a product of the fast-food environment. He was comfortable grabbing a hamburger for lunch and, when taking a client to dinner, never ventured beyond ordering a well-done steak and beer. In Europe, social graces count for more in the business environment. Most Europeans understand an American's ineptitude with wine lists and social graces and make allowances. However, in Bill's case, rather than attempting to learn, he belittled the customs themselves—attempted to impose his cultural values rather than live with those he encountered.

- Europe has a strong sense of history and a pervading tradition of nationalism. Bill was a product of the U.S. educational system. He knew numbers and statistics, but his sense of historical perspective became fuzzy at the Korean War and lapsed into nothingness before World War II. Bill was also a businessman—a capitalist, a believer in doing it yourself and not relying on governments and institutions. Europe is much more socialistic than the United States. Many Europeans are articulate spokesmen not only for socialism but also for the historical arguments as to its necessity. Bill's lack of knowledge of European history caused him to make blunders when dealing with nationalism. Bill thought all Europeans were the same. A quick overview of history would have told him that there is no real Europe. It is simply a geographical designation for a number of highly nationalistic entities.

- Bill came out even worse in his political discussions. His European colleagues assumed that since he was a top manager, he would be able to discuss broad issues such as socialism versus capitalism with some degree of knowledge. Bill, a product of the American educational system, did not have this knowledge and, rather than admitting it and keeping his mouth shut, tried to "wing it" on his own. The result of his bluff was a greater lack of credibility among his European colleagues.

The real tragedy of this situation was that Bill could have been saved from ruining his career. With proper expatriation selection and orientation techniques, he would have been weeded out and a more culturally adaptive person sent to Brussels.

There are Bills of varying degrees in every multinational company. One finds them in nearly every country, and they are not all from the United States. Many of them manage to grind out an overseas assignment, but what is the cost? Certainly the Bills of the world do not generate maximum productivity. How do you factor in the cost of alienating national employees in their host countries? And what happens to their careers once they return, even if they do bite the bullet for the entire term of their overseas assignment?

People are not machines that will work in any country. They are people and need to be selected with care. The simple fact that one has done all right in the United States is no guarantee that he will do all right in a different culture.

"Treat Him Like an American"

The scene is the West Coast headquarters of a worldwide high-technology company. It is late in the afternoon and an all-day conference involving the personnel director and the vice president of international operations is in progress. Ties are askew, ashtrays have enough cigarette butts to give a dinosaur lung cancer, and tempers are short.

What is the problem? The problem is Pierre. He has stormed the corporate offices and nailed his thesis on the international vice president's door. He wants more money, retroactive participation in French profit sharing, longer vacations, expatriate premiums, home leave provisions, tax protection, and a total compensation and benefit package that will make him better off than his boss, the American vice president of international operations.

Who is Pierre? He is not just another militant employee off the assembly line. Pierre is a key executive two levels from the top of the organization and heretofore regarded as a comer headed for a key top management position in the United States upon conclusion of his current assignment.

How did Pierre get in this fix? He was hired in Paris and managed the French subsidiary until it achieved significant market penetration in France. One day Pierre woke up and found that the job had lost challenge. There was nowhere for him to go. He was a big fish in a small pond. About the same time the company was beginning operations in Australia. What better logic than to send Pierre from France to Australia to utilize his flair for building up the business. After he had opened up operations in Australia, there were vague plans to move him back to headquarters.

Pierre was a task-oriented man. For six months he left his family in Paris, took a flat in Sydney, and worked day and night, making only two brief return trips to France. Then he moved his family to Australia and the trouble began.

The problems started simply enough. How did he get paid? The French subsidiary wanted him off their books. "No problem," said the personnel director, "we will pay you like an American. After all, you work for an American company, so we will pay you in U.S. dollars."

Pierre received his first paycheck and could not believe it. When transferred to the U.S. scale, he made less money than in France. (Top management salaries in parts of Western Europe have reached parity and in many cases have surpassed their U.S. counterparts. This is not even considering benefits, which have historically been much better in Europe than in the United States.)

Pierre took the salary reduction in stride, primarily because he was too involved in building up the market area and did not have time to worry about it then. After his family had been there one month, the U.S. dollar was devalued and the Australian dollar revalued. Since Pierre used U.S. dollars to buy Australian dollars, his purchasing power was cut.

The problems then increased in intensity. There was the matter of taxes. He was in Australia and legally responsible for Australian taxes. But Pierre's Australian taxes were more than he would have paid had he stayed in Paris. The first of many cables was sent to corporate headquarters.

"What about my salary and taxes?"

"Pay him like an American, tax him like an American!" said the personnel director.

The next round of cables soon followed. "But I am not an American; I am a Frenchman. I want a French salary and French tax levels, and while I'm at it, what about my French profit sharing? Do I lose this while in Australia?" (In France, many companies set aside, at least by U.S. standards, a rather liberal amount of money for profit sharing.) "What about my company car?" (This is another European custom for top management.) "How about vacation?" (Holidays in France are longer.) "How about home leave? When can I go back to France?"

As if this were not enough, further cables kept rolling in. "What about housing? I pay more for housing in Sydney than I did in Paris."

Then there was education. Who would pay the fee for correspondence courses to keep Pierre's children involved in the French educational system?

The crowning blow was when Pierre asked for a cost-of-living allowance. "It couldn't cost him more to live in Sydney than in Paris!" shouted the vice president of international operations. "What's happened to Pierre? He has turned into a greedy, me-first employee. Is this the kind of manager we want representing us overseas? Get him back here; let's talk this out now!"

Pierre gladly caught the next plane. How did all this happen? What caused Pierre's metamorphosis? It was another common fault of multinational companies engaging in the movement of people across borders. In the heat of battle decisions are made to move people without being thoroughly thought out. Moreover, these decisions are made without an underlying philosophy and plan.

In the past, Americans moving non-Americans from country to country could afford to be egocentric. Americans were the best paid, at least in base salary. Things have changed rapidly. American managers are no longer the highest paid in the world. Salaries in northern and western Europe have passed them. Professional managers in Mexico, Canada, and Australia are rapidly overtaking their U.S. counterparts. Furthermore, most non-U.S. countries have always had better benefits.

Taxes? What good are high salaries and benefits if the recipients have to pay them away in exorbitant income taxes? This has been a pat rationale in the "pay them like an

American" philosophy. American managers have had to take another look. In places like France and Switzerland the base income tax rates are not all that different. Some countries do not have capital gains taxes. In others, the tax laws and their enforcement are totally different. Even in high-tax countries, like the United Kingdom, Scandinavia, and Australia, there are government programs that are not available in the United States. Then consider the standard payment-in-kind techniques such as company cars, interest-free mortgages, and trips abroad for the family as well as the manager, all of which are designed to give the individual a lower reportable income than he actually experiences. If you add all this together, it is not difficult to see why Pierre would not be overjoyed at the prospect of being treated like an American.

Then, of course, there is culture. Pierre is French, he thinks French, eats French when he can, and speaks French. Certainly, he can speak English; many American companies equate linguistic ability with the acceptance of American cultural values. This is a fallacy. Unlike the American, who for the most part demands that his foreign business contacts speak his language, Pierre and our foreign neighbors study our language and speak it as a matter of business convenience.

Once again, there are a number of Pierres in the world. The naive ones either accept the system or return to their home country and plateau. The wily ones, those who have experience, begin negotiating special deals. In many cases, one can find two countrymen working in another country with radically different provisions.

Neither alternative is desirable. The multinational employer needs a consistent expatriation philosophy. Treating all expatriates like Americans neither is philosophically sound nor makes business sense. In the next chapter we shall examine philosophical alternatives related to international people moves.

TO THE EXPATRIATE

Before rushing off to purchase your air tickets, give some thought to why you were selected. Was it because you were a star in your home country? Was that the only reason? Did anyone give any consideration to your cultural adaptivity? If not, you had better! Give some consideration to Bill—his problems—why he crashed. How much of Bill can you find in yourself?

You may, indeed, have a fast track record, but how will the skills that got you where you are help you in your new assignment? Do not necessarily think your boss or your personnel manager can help. Have they ever worked overseas?

Before getting on that plane, read the rest of this book, particularly the sections on selection and orientation. If both you and your company measure up, great, you will have a good assignment. If you have doubts, think hard. Is an international assignment worth the personal and career trauma you may experience? Furthermore, if you find yourself in the position of a Pierre, do not let your desire to succeed allow you to forget your cultural bias. Everyone has cultural bias; yours will pop out sooner or later. Before you take that assignment, find out your company's philosophy. You too are invited to read the remainder of this book, concentrating on the sections on philosophy and compensation.

13

Part 2

PHILOSOPHY

Chapter 2

PHILOSOPHICAL FOUNDATIONS

Structuralist Approach

In an age of rapid technological and social change, many managers have adopted a freewheeling, even swashbuckling, approach to their job. It is in style for managers to speak of "solving problems" rather than "administering rules." One fast-moving executive categorizes all staff functions as "going to the manual." No matter what the problem, they have a manual (a set of rules) to solve it. If the answer is not in the manual, his perception of staff mentality is that they will quickly write one in order that the problem may be solved.

While it is true that the rules administrators of the world have tended to let the manual get in the way of the solution, many managers have overreacted. In a great many situations, problem solving has occurred without any attempt to codify decisions to insure internal equity for future decisions. What is needed is a swashbuckling manager with a sword in one hand and a manual in the other. Nowhere is this more true than in the international movement of people.

International transfers are by far a company's most complex people transaction. What is involved is not just simple base compensation or benefits but an employee's entire life style. Decisions in this area need to be grounded in a consistent, equitable, and codified philosophy.

Anyone who has been involved in international people problems knows the tremendous latitude, even within the most structured system, for exercising creativity and problem solving. These same individuals will testify to the essential need for a clear philosophical base from which to view international transfers. As we shall see, without such a base and supportive codification in the form of policies and procedures, it becomes impossible to explain to foreign service employees the basis upon which they are paid, taxed, housed, and returned to their home country. Without a clear structuralist approach, international transfers soon become hopelessly bogged down in hip-shooting decisions that form their own philosophical precedents. Such a situation is unhealthy for both the company and the employee.

"It Is Not the Same as Sending a Man to California"

The first foundation that needs clarification is the difference between transfers *within* a country and transfers *between* countries. This may appear, on first glance, to be an easy differentiation; however, a number of sophisticated multinational companies have experienced varying degrees of headaches as a result of failure to understand the differences. Let us eavesdrop to the beginning of a long lunch in a New York restaurant:

> Director of production for a heavy-equipment manufacturer to his personnel vice president: "I'm going to send Henry to Holland to head up our new manufacturing facility. Then I'm going to send John to take his place in California. Do you see any problem with these two moves?"
>
> "When you send a man to Holland, it's different from sending someone to California. It requires a whole different set of selection, orientation, and compensation

tools," responded the personnel man, sitting back and preparing for a long lunch. "It just is not the same as sending a man to California."

"Well, I really can't see the difference," said the production director. "Move one man to California and move another to Holland. A transfer is a transfer, right?"

Wrong! These are the kinds of generalizations that make experienced international managers shudder. In the above example, the personnel vice president ordered another martini and set about explaining the differences.

It is important for the manager involved in sending people overseas to recognize the differences between an intra- and an intercountry transfer. Some of the obvious differences are as follows:

- Many intracountry transfers, particularly within large countries such as the United States, are classified as permanent. There may be an eventual fuzzy scheme to return the transferee to the company's headquarters city for a promotion, but there is often nothing guaranteed.

- When most companies ask a family to move from Chicago to Dallas, it is intended that Dallas be its home, at least for the foreseeable future. If, however, the same family moves to Tokyo, it is, at least for most multinationals, a planned return or expatriation assignment, and the family faces a number of different problems than if it had moved to Dallas. The transferee may not choose to sell his home in Chicago and, certainly, cannot afford to buy one in Tokyo. There will be no cost-of-living allowance in Dallas, while any American in his right mind will ask for one in Tokyo. The transferee to Dallas will not get a home leave to reacquaint himself with the Chicago culture, while if he were to go to Tokyo, he most certainly should have one.

- Then there is the entire matter of culture and language. While a dyed-in-the-wool resident of Chicago may indeed find cultural differences in Dallas, they are not nearly so great as the differences one would find in moving from Chicago to Tokyo. These cultural differences tug at an expatriate in hundreds of subtle ways not experienced in intracountry transfers.

A foundation of any rational method of international people planning takes into account the differences between intra- and intercountry moves. These transfers are substantially different and demand different tools. The person transferring from Germany to the United Kingdom needs different treatment than the person transferring from Frankfurt to Munich. The American moving to Bangkok needs different treatment than someone moving to Cleveland. This fundamental concept, simple though it may be, needs to be communicated, understood, and codified in order to form a foundation of a rational expatriate system.

Look Before You Leap

A second foundation of any systematic international people movement system is an examination of the reasons for sending someone to work in another country in the first place. This basic question is often overlooked by companies in their rush to purchase their employees' international plane tickets.

In the past, many American multinationals simply assumed that Americans must fill key jobs in other countries. By definition, Americans would do a better job than local nationals. Thus, the focus of the decision was who to send rather than why send an American at all. One does not have to look very deep to expose the invalidity of this concept. Not only is it untrue on the surface (Americans are not by definition better managers) but also the increasing nationalism and desire for local ownership make many American top managers counterproductive when compared with nationals.

Why then do companies send people from one country to work in another? The following are some of the invalid reasons:

Historical accident—"But we've always had an expatriate do that job."

Egocentric nationalism—"But no one can manage that operation except an American."

Political maneuvering—"If we send Joe out of the country, we don't have to worry about his being in contention for the next job. By the time he gets back, we'll have things fixed so that he hasn't a chance of running the operation."

Path of least resistance—"It's too hard to worry about hiring a Frenchman to do a job in France. We don't even know how to hire one, let alone what or how to pay him. Let's just send an American over and be done with it." This particular solution is not only common but also extremely costly, as most Americans sent on this type of assignment end up hiring a local to help them cope anyway, and the company not only has the expatriate's cost but also the national's cost.

Some of the more logical reasons are as follows:

Specific "fire-fighting" assignment—"We'll send Fred over to supervise the installation of the new computer. He'll train a local to maintain it and be back in less than two years."

Developmental assignment—"Jim has a great deal of experience in the domestic market. If he had a feel for the international market, he would be in a good position to take the vice president's job when Ed retires in five years. Let's send him overseas to manage our international operation with the specific plan to give him Ed's job if he is successful."

Training assignment—"Let's bring Hans over from the Hague to spend three years in headquarters. Then we'll send him back to Holland as our country manager, but first he needs to be trained in corporate policies and procedures, specifically, our accounting system."

Specific management assignment—"The Italian sales-manager's position is too small in scope to support a local. Let's send Nick from our Greek operation to manage sales in Italy. We want to investigate consolidation of the two operations anyway, and it makes sense to have Nick manage Italian sales so he can help us decide what to do."

It is important that managers concerned with moving people across borders assess the validity of their objectives in sending an expatriate. Why do they need them? Is it worth the cost? What are the alternatives? In any international system these questions need to be addressed early in the international people movement sequence.

Organizational Dimensions

A third philosophical foundation of any international people movement system is organizational in nature. Some corporations have international divisions; others do not. Some, like the State Department, rotate foreign service employees in and out of overseas assignments for most of their careers. When an employee takes one overseas assignment, he can logically expect to be given many more. He may, in fact, be rotated back to his home country, but this may be only a temporary assignment before being assigned overseas again.

Other companies pluck employees from domestic assignments for relatively short periods of time and return them to their home country with little chance of their getting another overseas assignment. Within this philosophy, most overseas assignments are specific in nature and in a project mode.

Still other corporations operate a hybrid system. They have no international division, but they have a cadre of employees who tend to get more than one international assignment even though each is specific in nature.

It is crucial that organizations sending people on international assignments understand the organizational dimensions of their decisions. If a company does not have this part of its philosophy ironed out, it is in for real trouble as there are implications in compensation, benefits, development, and, certainly, in the selection of the foreign service employee.

Fall-Back Position

A consistent and clearly understood philosophy gives multinational managers a base to fall back upon when confronted with complex people situations, as illustrated by the following examples.

Teddy's Tax Troubles

Teddy was a high-rolling sales manager transferred to a Latin American country with dubious enforcement of its tax laws. Teddy's firm, a neophyte in the multinational people movement business, sent him south with little preparation.

Historically, expatriates from Teddy's firm had not paid any local taxes while on assignment in Latin America. Since they were outside the United States for the right period of time, they also were excluded from paying U.S. taxes on most of their income. Unfortunately, during Teddy's assignment, the Latin American government turned loose its new tax agents (trained and modeled after the U.S. Internal Revenue Service) and they caught Teddy. Before he could leave the country, he had to pay back taxes for the three years of his assignment. Since the tax rates in this country were much higher than those in the United States, Teddy screamed to his U.S. boss.

"It isn't my obligation; the company put me down here. They have to pay the back taxes!"

Teddy's company was also startled when it received retroactive tax audits on the last three Americans who had been assigned to this country. What should it do? Whose obligation was it?

If Teddy had not been discovered by the local taxing authorities, he would have gained on both ends. (No taxes in Latin America and most of his income tax free in the United States.) Now that Teddy's case had surfaced, the company was in trouble in two areas: Its business contacts, primarily the government itself, were not happy, and it also was faced with deciding whether it was, at least morally, liable for its employee's tax evasion.

Teddy's company badly needed a philosophy when it came to taxes. Before Teddy even left for his foreign assignment, the company's tax philosophy should have been communicated and understood. The following are brief examples of tax philosophies:

- Tax equalization—Companies utilizing this philosophy tell their employees that they will pay no more and no less income taxes than they would have paid if they had remained in their home country. The company then assesses each employee an approximate tax and takes care of all tax obligations for the employee.

- Tax protection—The company guarantees that an expatriate will pay no more tax than if he had remained in his home country, but allows him to gain from any lower tax levels.

- Tax minimization—The company and the employee work together to help lower the expatriate's income tax obligation and the company's obligation to keep the employee whole. There are some countries where schemes such as splitting income for reporting purposes are legal and tax minimization is a valid concept. Some companies, however, have the philosophy of helping the employee lower his tax obligation even where the legality of doing so is suspect. This is definitely not advocated, since the company may place the employee in the position of signing a false tax return. Would you want to work for a company with such a philosophy?

Another example of the importance of a philosophy as a fall-back position is the relationship of tax and salary levels. This can be illustrated by the reluctant Englishman.

The Reluctant Englishman

Trevor was an employee from Liverpool who spent five years working in the United States for a worldwide consulting engineering firm. While in the United States, Trevor was paid as an American, and he paid U.S. taxes. He also paid Social Security taxes and participated in the company's U.S. retirement plan. Trevor was slated to return to his home country to head up his company's operations there.

"I bloody well won't go," shouted Trevor to the personnel manager. "I can't live on an English salary, nor can I afford to pay those horrible tax rates. The only way I'll go is as an American."

The head of international operations found it hard to believe that an Englishman would return to England only as a U.S. expatriate, and Trevor was ordered to go "or else!" Trevor chose the "or else," left the company, and remained in the United States. But now he works for a competitor.

Trevor's former company now has an expatriate philosophy. It would have been much cheaper to adopt one before it lost a key man. A company with a philosophy would, no doubt, have been concerned about Trevor's eventual repatriation. It would, perhaps, have kept him in the retirement plan in the United Kingdom and given him home leaves to keep him culturally attuned to his home country. His salary could at least have been quoted two ways—his British salary in pounds and the U.S. equivalent. That way it would have been clear to Trevor that he was living on a false standard. The tax problem is a sticky one with British expatriates. Again, however, communication of his temporary status might have helped. Above all, a proper replacement and repatriation planning system might have indicated that five years was far too long for Trevor to remain in the United States. Perhaps nine months to a year would have accomplished the training without his becoming addicted to U.S. tax and salary levels.

Definitions

The literature on international transfers is inconsistent in its use of terms. Since it is important when discussing philosophy that the basic terms have a common meaning, the following will establish working definitions of some of the more common terms:

- *Expatriate*—This is a generic term for anyone working outside his home country with a planned return to that or a third country. There are two subdivisions of this general term: *Non-U.S.* is an individual working in one country outside the United States who will eventually return to a home country outside the United States. (Some firms still have different policies for U.S. and non-U.S. expatriates, and thus have the need to differentiate.) *U.S.* is an employee of a U.S. company (usually a U.S. citizen) who is working in another country with a plan to return to the United States.

- *Foreign service employee*—This term means the same as expatriate, although it has organizational connotations. (A person joins an international division and spends much of his career in the "foreign service" part of the business.)

- *Home country*—This is the expatriate's normal country of residence; where he originally came from and will eventually return to.

- *Host country*—This is the country in which an expatriate is working.

- *Third-country national*—This is a specialized type of expatriate living in a third country. For example, if an individual is transferred from Country A to Country B, he is an expatriate. If, however, the individual is subsequently transferred to Country C with plans to return to Country A, he is a third-country national. This is a rather academic definition. In actual practice, many U.S. multinationals refer to anyone who transfers from one country to another outside the United States as a third-country national. (In these cases non-U.S. expatriate means the same thing.)

From the Foundations

In this chapter we have explored the philosophical foundations of an international people movement system. In the next chapter we will build upon these foundations by examining some evolving trends and tracing their use in a replacement and repatriation planning system.

Chapter 3

APPLIED PHILOSOPHY

Evolving Trends

The philosophical foundations described in the previous chapter serve as an anchor to the evolving trends of expatriation philosophy. This chapter will trace some of these trends and will examine their reflection in a replacement and repatriation planning system. The evolving trends in international transfers are as follows:

- Stricter definitions—Companies can no longer afford to hip shoot their expatriation policies. There are too many people and too much money involved. Even the most swinging nonstructured company is becoming more concerned with the rules administration approach to expatriation.

- Diminishing number of "career" internationalists— Expatriation is becoming more and more expensive. Organizations are finding that Americans are not always the ideal nationality and, in fact, that there may not be a perfect nationality. Organizations are changing rapidly, and the multinational company is at the forefront of this change. More and more multinationals are moving away from the foreign service career concept.

- More short-term specific assignments—As the number of career internationalists diminishes, the number of short-term specific assignments is on the increase. There are many more fire-fighting and specific training assignments than in the past.

- Development of strong national organizations with local management—The days of the colonialist expatriate manager are numbered. Many expatriates now report to local nationals in their host country. Local managers, properly trained, just do better despite what some culturally biased American managers believe.

- Relating an expatriate to his home country—The more sophisticated expatriate systems relate an individual's pay, benefits, and, if possible, culture to his home country. This makes subsequent moves much easier and gives an understandable fall-back position.

- Better international manpower planning—The more sophisticated multinationals attempt to define not only the reason for an expatriate assignment but also the position the expatriate will assume in his next assignment.

Godfather System*

Philosophy is only as good as its application, at least in the hard-boiled world of the multinational enterprise. The time has come, therefore, to take the principles we have thus far examined and frame them in a specific system.

The remainder of this chapter deals with the godfather system. This system not only gives an example of one method of structuring a replacement and repatriation planning

*Adapted from David M. Noer, "Integrating Foreign Service Employees to Home Organization: The Godfather Approach," *Personnel Journal*, 1974, *53* (No. 1), 45-51. Copyright 1974 by Personnel Journal, Inc.

system but, more important, illustrates the practicality of institutionalizing the philosophies of international transfers.

In order to understand the godfather system, it is necessary to review the problems with which it attempts to deal. These are as follows:

- Big-fish-in-small-pond syndrome—Many expatriates function at a higher level, although in a smaller arena, while overseas. Upon return they find themselves a medium-sized fish in a bigger pond which results in frustration and trauma. This is also true on the social level with the wives. Many international assignments expose wives to business-oriented entertainment at a social plateau that they find appealing when compared to the normal hausfrau existence they experience upon repatriation.

- Organizational changes—Most multinational companies have a constantly shifting organizational structure. The returning expatriate often finds himself in a totally different organizational culture when he returns to his home organization, and his cultural shock is sometimes more severe than that which he experienced on his foreign assignment.

- Job security—A potential expatriate can experience living patterns abroad on vacations or extended business travel without having to risk job security by accepting an overseas assignment and insulating himself from promotional opportunities in his home organization. Potential expatriates hear horror stories about employees returning from foreign assignments with no jobs back in their home organizations.

In some cases, managers still regard returning expatriates as having had their day in the sun and are not sympathetic toward finding positions for them. Many returned expatriates end up on assignments that do not utilize the skills gained while overseas. Still others become frustrated and quit, leaving the company with no return on its investment.

- Cost of maintaining expatriates overseas—Expatriates are expensive. International personnel and accounting functions are becoming increasingly sophisticated in their ability to track the total cost of expatriates. Base salaries, when combined with expatriate premiums, home leave costs, and tax equalization expenses, dictate increasing concern over the manpower-planning dimensions of expatriation assignments.

The implications of these problems are clear. International managers must become more involved in the manpower-planning aspects of international people moves—in particular, with repatriation and replacement planning. The godfather system is an attempt to do this on a systematic basis, as shown by the following presentation:

GODFATHER	EXPATRIATE
Is in expatriate's country of next assignment.	Knows where he is going next and for whom he will work.
Is responsible for securing a position for expatriate when he returns.	Knows probable job on return.
Is responsbile for assuring that replacement plan is implemented.	Motivated to work toward replacement plan (may be judged accordingly).
Is focal point for communications.	Has one person who "cares."

Components of a Godfather System

It must be intended that the expatriate eventually returns to another country (usually his home country) at the conclusion of his assignment. A company should not only define the type of position that the expatriate will assume upon his return but also designate an individual who will be responsible for assuring that the repatriation takes place in an orderly and nontraumatic manner.

This individual maintains an umbilical cord relationship to the expatriate during his assignment. The individual designated as the godfather is generally the manager to whom the expatriate will report upon conclusion of his assignment.

Before the expatriate leaves for a foreign assignment, a specific plan for replacing him is generated. When is it intended that he come back? Who will replace him on a foreign assignment? A local national (this is the trend)? If so, what are the training plans for the local national? What is the training? If it is another expatriate, why—who—when?

The following are three major categories of assignments in which the godfather concept can work.

Replacement by a Local National—Expatriate Judged by His Ability to Replace Himself

A bank headquartered in New York has a need for a U.S. expatriate to run a branch bank in Paris. It is intended that the U.S. expatriate selected be replaced by a local national. Before the U.S. expatriate leaves, the following happens: (a) The position to which he will return is defined. He is assigned a godfather (the individual to whom he will report when he returns). (b) A repatriation plan is generated. It is thought that it will take two years to train a Frenchman to assume the expatriate's duties. (c) A specific replacement plan is defined, including the training required of the local national replacement, any short training assignments to the United States, and other experiences the local national needs in order to qualify him to replace the expatriate. (d) The U.S. expatriate is then judged by his ability to replace

himself by a local national. The following order represents
this process:

> Need for expatriate defined.
>> "Best" nationality determined.
>>> Expatriate selected.
>>>> Probable job upon repatriation determined.
>>>> Godfather assigned.
>>>>> Replacement plan developed (expatriate responsible for hiring and training local national to take his place).
>>>>>> Expatriate goes overseas.
>>>>>>> Expatriate hires and develops foreign national.
>>>>>>> Foreign national assumes duties.
>>>>>>>> Expatriate returns to home country to assume next job.

Replacement by Another Expatriate

A large electronics firm has a need for an individual to
be expatriated to Belgium to assume broad general management functions throughout Europe. The candidate is a
Frenchman. Before he leaves Paris the following happens: (a)
He is assigned a godfather. In this case it is a top executive
in the United States. It is intended that upon conclusion of
his Brussels assignment, he will not return to Paris, because
if he does so he will be taking a downgrading, but rather go
on to the United States for a general management position.
(b) The duration of his assignment is defined as five years. It
is intended that he be replaced by a manager from the
United States. The responsibility for selecting and training
this replacement is given to the individual to whom the
Frenchman will report at the conclusion of his assignment.
In this case, the godfather has responsibility for the
replacement and the repatriation plan. The following order
represents this process:

Need for expatriate defined.
  "Best" nationality determined.
    Expatriate selected.
      Next job determined—not in home country but in a
      third country.
        Godfather assigned in third country.
          Replacement responsibility defined in third
          country.
            Expatriate goes to new assignment.
              Replacement sent over.
                Expatriate goes to third country to assume
                next job.

One-Time Assignment—No Replacement

A construction company has contracted to build an apartment complex in Eastern Europe. A U.S. expatriate is needed to manage the project. An individual is selected. Before he leaves, the following happens: (a) The position to which he will return is defined, and a godfather is assigned. (b) The length of assignment is determined, and there is no replacement plan generated. The following order represents this process:

Need for expatriate defined.
  "Best" nationality determined.
    Expatriate selected.
      Probable next job determined.
        Godfather assigned.
          No replacement plan developed.
            Expatriate goes overseas.
              Expatriate returns to assume next job.

Tools of a Godfather System

Perhaps the most effective tool in order to make this system work in a highly complex multinational company with large numbers of expatriates is a *replacement and repatriation planning report*. This report, generated on a regularly scheduled basis, lists all expatriates, the degree of penetration into their assignment, the name of the manager with repatriation responsibility (the godfather), and the name of the manager with replacement responsibility. The individual expatriate, the godfather, and the individual with replacement plan responsibility receive regular updates of this document. It is a constant reminder to the godfather that he has an individual overseas for whom he is responsible. It reminds the individual with replacement responsibility that he is being held accountable for replacing the expatriate. It tends to reassure the expatriate that he has not been forgotten.

Another tool of the godfather system is *planned communications* with the expatriate. Company newsletters, news about the department to which the individual will be repatriating, and other communications are generated through the godfather, who sends them to the expatriate. The structure of this communications plan can vary among companies or operating units within companies. It is, however, important that the godfather be involved with the communications to the expatriate.

It is inherent in the system that the godfather be held *accountable* for implementing the repatriation plan. It is also essential that the individual responsible for implementing the replacement plan be held accountable for its implementation.

The godfather system not only is relatively simple to set up but also alleviates a number of concerns held by the modern expatriate. Under this system, the expatriate knows the type of position he will be assuming upon repatriation, has a strong umbilical cord to the country of his next assignment, and, if given the replacement planning responsibility, is motivated to replace himself with a local national.

The godfather system is an example of an effective replacement and repatriation planning system. However, the system is only as good as the people who make it work. A company can have the most sophisticated system in existence and it will fall flat on its face without the right

expatriates. The key to any international people system is
the selection of the basic ingredient—the expatriate. How
are expatriates selected? What are the pitfalls? Turn to
Chapter 4.

TO THE EXPATRIATE

In the past your company's philosophy may just have been a few dusty platitudes serving as a preamble to a policy manual, but things will change when you cross that border. Your company's expatriate philosophy will become very vivid when viewed in the context of an international assignment. Your company's philosophy will dictate how you are paid, housed, and taxed on one level; on another, it is your company's philosophy that will make you excited or bitter once you are overseas.

Start with the assumption that your company has an obligation to clearly communicate its philosophy to you—after all, it is dealing with your life. If no one brings it up, ask! Try your personnel manager or the head of international operations. If you get blank looks and meaningless mutterings, chances are you are off to a bad start on your international assignment. If, however, you are given logical answers that relate back to the foundations in Chapter 2 and the evolving trends in Chapter 3, you are fortunate; you work for a company that understands the value of a philosophy.

The potential expatriate should ask himself the following questions before accepting an international assignment:

- What is your company's approach to rules administration? Does it have any at all? Who administrates them? What are they? If there is a structured set of policies and procedures dealing with international moves, you should feel good. If not, well . . . best have your boss read Chapter 2. Determine the rules, discuss them with someone, and make sure everyone understands what will happen to you when you are abroad. The company should take the initiative in communications; if not, you must. Once you are over there things get snarled under the best circumstances. Take some time before you go. Adopt a structuralist approach even if your company does not. There is plenty of opportunity for swashbuckling once you are overseas. Take it slow and according to the rules until everyone understands the terms and conditions of your assignment.

- Why are they sending you over in the first place? Run through the list of reasons in Chapter 2. Do any of them fit? If you accept an international assignment for the wrong reasons, it can not only ruin your career but also have long-range effects on your life outside the job. Better be sure you know and agree with the reasons you are being sent overseas.

- Do you understand your company's international organization? You would be amazed at the number of heretofore mature and conservative employees who, caught in the euphoria of an international transfer, fail to make a realistic assessment of a simple thing like how long they are expected to stay and what will happen to them upon their return. What is your company's organizational philosophy? Are you making the first step toward a career expatriate assignment, or just taking a brief side trip from your main career path?

- What is your company's tax and pay philosophy? How are you paid? In what currency? When? Does your company expect you to split your pay? Why? Is it legal? What does it do with taxes? Who does the work? Are you expected to keep records?

- What kind of a manpower-planning system does your company have? What does it expect you to do about a replacement in your host country? Is it a real philosophy or is it just someone's dream? Better get it in writing; people change in home country organizations. If your company does not have a structured approach, it is up to you to work one out for yourself.

- What happens when you return? Talk to someone who has come back. Does your company reward, punish, or ignore returned expatriates? If you do it right, you will have one of the most difficult jobs in your career while overseas. Does anyone in your company know that? If you do your job right, can you expect to return to a hero's welcome or to a reorganized operation where you will have to scramble for a job?

Part 3

SELECTION

Chapter 4

BEHAVIORAL DIMENSIONS

"If you think it's hard to pick a person to move from Atlanta to New York, you ought to try selecting someone for Milan!" expounded the international accounting manager, reaching with increasing dependence for his third martini.

"First they've got to be able to do the job, which is hard enough to determine. Then they've got to want to move to Italy. And, as if that weren't enough, they've got to get along with our Italian management team!"

This manager was verbalizing one of the most important and frustrating dimensions of the international people business—selection. In addition to the normal one-country selection criteria, a number of unique characteristics also need to be assessed for international assignments. Any international selection system should be geared to respond to the following behavioral dimensions.

Cultural Adaptivity

The ability to accomplish work in a different cultural environment not only takes into account cultural awareness and sensitivity but also demands the ability to work in an unstructured environment when compared to "the way things were done at home." Selection tools need to be established to measure this dimension. From a psychological viewpoint, they need to be validated and made reliable. Some multinationals have begun to experiment in this area. Unfortunately, many others simply ignore the need for measuring and assessing cultural adaptivity. This is an extremely important dimension and one in which much more effort is needed when selecting people for international moves.

Entrepreneurial Characteristics

A successful international transferee and his or her family should look upon the move as an adventure as opposed to a sentence. The author is familiar with a case where the highlight in the daily life of an expatriate and his family was the circling of a calendar each evening when the employee returned home. He and his family gathered around the calendar and marked off another day of his international assignment, only in his case it was not an assignment, it was a sentence; it did not last the length of time intended but was cut short by his on-the-job failure. A postmortem indicated that the failure was due to his inelastic personality and his family's inability to cope with the foreign environment.

Most successful international moves are looked upon as adventures by the incumbents. On the business level, the expatriate should be a risk taker, able to function in an unstructured environment. Most multinational firms are continually changing. This flux is nowhere more evident than in the international environment. A risk taker, an employee with an entrepreneurial bent, is most comfortable and effective in an overseas assignment.

The same principle holds true on a nonwork level. The most common household decisions—calling the plumber, getting the car repaired, or shopping for a special cut of meat—take quantum jumps in levels of complexity when performed in an international environment.

The person approaching these problems as an entrepreneur will find them not only exciting but their solutions self-actualizing. The person looking upon them as a vexing task will tend to become involved in continual bouts of the expatriate syndrome* which will only cause the problems to heighten and the anxiety to increase.

Selection must, therefore, address an expatriate's risk-taking ability. Has he exhibited entrepreneurial characteristics? What have his living patterns been in the past? How, either on the job or off the job, have these characteristics been demonstrated? The perception of an international assignment as an entrepreneurial experience is not widespread among multinational firms. It is, however, a dimension that needs further research by the behavioral scientists and consideration when making selection decisions.

Off-the-Job Behavioral Patterns

In the past, selection within one country in many cases has ignored the importance of what the employee does off the job. In fact, the trend is to emphasize on-the-job characteristics and not address off-the-job behavioral patterns. This trend is accentuated by the work force demand for privacy. However, off-the-job behavior—family, social, and recreational patterns—is important when considering candidates for international assignments. Families are suddenly cut off from traditional recreational and social patterns. What they do on weekends—now that the husband cannot play golf, the wife cannot visit her mother, or the children cannot go to summer camp—becomes much more important. The selection implications are obvious. It is important to assure that an international transferee has a realistic expectation of what will happen to his life style when he transfers.

All family members involved in a transfer need to understand this aspect of an international assignment. In

---

*An expatriate illness characterized by wallowing in self-pity because "this isn't the way they do things back home."

many countries, the expatriate's wife will be expected to do business entertaining much more often. Does she want to do this? Can she do this? What will this do to her image as a liberated person?

In some countries the basics are hard. Simple things such as buying clothes or taking a subway become major problems. The whole area of off-the-job behavior and its importance to a successful international move needs to be explored, assessed, and explained by those involved in international selection.

A Challenge to Behavioral Scientists

More hard data in the area of international selection are needed. Psychologists looking for areas in which to do research need look no further. There is a surprising lack of validated research on international selection. The above areas are offered based upon experiential data; however, more research is needed.

With the importance of international assignments, both from a monetary and developmental viewpoint, the next generation should produce some meaningful behavioral research which will help eliminate the shadows of uncertainty and conjecture involved in international people selection.

Toward a Better Union

An expatriate assignment can be one of the most challenging and rewarding business and personal experiences a person will go through or it can be a horrible experience; there does not seem to be any middle ground. It is incumbent upon the multinational employer to do everything possible to make selection decisions that will predispose expatriates to a positive experience. To that end, this chapter has suggested a behavioral frame of reference for international selection. The next chapter offers some specific guidelines.

Chapter 5

GUIDELINES FOR SELECTION

This chapter outlines some specific guidelines for selection. These guidelines can apply to new employees, who are selected to be sent directly on expatriate assignments, as well as to internal transferees, who in most multinational companies make up the bulk of the international people traffic.

Know Your Cultural Bias

All of us make decisions based on our culture—what we wear, what we eat, if we marry, whom we marry, how we work—all are culturally derived. Selection is no different. We make employment decisions based on cultural values.

International selection decisions are affected not only by the culture from which we make our decisions but also by the culture into which the expatriate is assigned. The cultural aspects of decision making are also affected by the fact that culture is dynamic. The work ethic of the 40–50-year-old middle manager is certainly different from that of the new graduate entering the labor market.

The dynamic nature of cultural values works at both ends of an international assignment. The German manager brought up in the aftermath of World War II has different cultural values from the young German worker. A 28-year-old U.S. technician selected by a 45-year-old middle manager in the United States and sent to work for a 50-year-old manager in Germany, where the peer group is 28-year-old German technicians, is caught in the crossfire of cultural values before he starts. If he and the individual who selected him are unaware of cultural differences and cultural bias, the chances for a cultural clash are greatly increased.

A key rule for multinational selection is to know your cultural bias. Attempt to understand the value system behind your company's work ethic. Does your company, for example, reward conservative clean-cut businessmen? You should also know what the cultural system is in your foreign organization. If all of your future expatriate's co-workers have long hair, wear beards, and enjoy long wine-dominated lunches, at the very least you should prepare him for these differences.

If you, like one prominent multinational, are headquartered in New York and have New York cultural values, you might tend to select the most successful New Yorker to go to Bangkok. If after six months you have a problem with the perception of your manager among the Thai nationals ("he is rude, pushy, and overly competitive"), you might have to look no further than your cultural selection criteria. In Thailand courtesy, patience, and decorum are cultural values.

Selection must take into account cultural bias. Since we are all to a degree culturally blind, it is wise to attempt to have an individual from the culture to which the expatriate will be assigned become involved in the selection decision— at least in an advisory capacity. This individual should not, however, be in the reporting chain of the expatriate selected. A foreign national occupying this position cannot afford to be overly objective. What happens, for example, if he concludes that the potential expatriate manager is culturally insensitive and will have a difficult time coping with the local environment, and he tells this to what amounts to his boss's boss who is making the selection decision? If the person is selected anyway or is told why he was not, the foreign national ends up in an unenviable position. It is much better to utilize a neutral evaluation. There are many qualified individuals from every conceivable country living within the United States. It is wise for individuals making international selection decisions to consider choosing one of them to help with the cultural aspects of selection. (These individuals can also be most helpful in an international orientation program.)

Select Within the Philosophical Ground Rules

Selection for an international assignment needs to take place within a company's philosophical ground rules. The necessity for a philosophy was discussed in Chapter 2. It is important that individuals making selection decisions know the philosophical system, particularly the reasons for sending an employee and the duration of the assignment.

A company, for example, may have a philosophy of short-term specific assignments. The selection system for these assignments would differ from companies having a philosophy of enlisting in an international division as a long-term career. One of the most sophisticated selection systems is utilized by a company which seldom sends people overseas longer than 18 months. This company becomes involved in cultural assessment, outside psychological assessment, including the family and advance trips, and a number of in-depth interviews with people who have been there. This particular company is part of a conglomerate which has another organization with the opposite philosophy—sending expatriates for long-term more-than-one-country assignments. These people are selected on the "he's the best in the U.S." criteria and put on the first plane. The result is short-term expatriations, which are relatively trouble free and successful, and long-term assignments, which are haphazard and costly. The lesson to be learned is to simply select within philosophical ground rules.

Communications must also follow the philosophy. If it is a short-term assignment, tell that to the individual before he accepts an offer. If there is no chance that the person will have another expatriation assignment, best tell him that before he accepts and travels overseas, gets entangled with the international community, and wonders why he has to come back to his home assignment in a year. If, on the other hand, a person is selected for an overseas assignment based on the probability of spending additional time as an expatriate in a third country and possibly spending a large part of his career living as an expatriate, the selection system should highlight this fact and communicate it to him in order to assure mutual understanding, otherwise he may wish to come home too soon.

If the expatriate is being judged on his ability to train a local national to take his place, then training ability should be part of the selection decision. A company may have the best godfather system going and may explain to an incumbent that he is being measured by his ability to train his replacement; if, however, the expatriate does not know how to train, the system falls apart. If training is part of an expatriation system philosophy, then an expatriate must be selected within this philosophy—he should have some training skills.

Know Your Country of Assignment

Any consultant will tell you that it is axiomatic that selection be geared to a specific job. In other words, one must have a job description in order to define a standard against which to select. This also holds true in international selection. Certainly, one must know the parameters of the position.

In addition to knowing what the job is, selection must also be geared to the country of assignment. In order to select an individual to go to any given country, one must know something about that country—how business is conducted and what its cultural norms are. This then leads the selector to some assumptions about the type of person who will be most likely to succeed in this environment.

An easy way to develop a data base on a country is to talk to people who have lived there, both as nationals and as expatriates. Most multinationals have internal people who have lived in almost every country to which they are assigning expatriates. There are also books on business and social customs and, of course, there are first-hand experiences gained by business travel.

If the company makes a "cold" selection, the cultural selection index will be zero. The company would be in the same boat as a recruiter interviewing candidates for an accounting position who cannot differentiate between an accountant and, say, an engineer, and who does not know what skills or duties are involved in the position.

While no cultural adjustment is easy, some are easier than others, and multinational jargon has evolved the terms "hard" or "easy" countries. For example, an American going to Australia would certainly have to make cultural adjustments; however, the adjustments would be no where near as severe as he would undergo if he were to go to Rumania. The culture, the language, and the economic systems are radically different.

It behooves the manager making international selection decisions to know the differences between countries and to factor this into the selection decision. Too many managers making selection decisions for expatriates perceive everything "over there" as the same, and a person who is an "international type" can just be sent anywhere.

Involve the Spouse

Wives, if the employees are male, husbands, if the employees are female, and dependent children have to live there too. Selecting someone to move overseas involves the family to a much greater degree than an intracountry transfer. ~~Many~~ failures have occurred because of the spouse's reluctance to transfer in the first place and the inability to adapt once in a host country. Many expatriates, who were predicted as having a marginal chance of success, have done very well because of supportive spouses. It is, therefore, important to factor spouse evaluation into an expatriate selection system.

Many companies are moving away from this concept when it comes to intracountry selection decisions. There are good and valid reasons why this should not be the case in international transfers. Consider the case of the manufacturing manager transferred to an East European country.

Maynard was sent to East Europe for an 18-month period. His job was to design a turnkey manufacturing operation within an agency of this East European country's government. Maynard was the first American sent to East Europe from his company. In fact, he was one of the first Americans to live in this country in recent times.

Maynard was an obvious candidate. He had good interpersonal skills and in-depth technical knowledge of the manufacturing process, and he looked upon the assignment as an adventure as well as a catapult into higher level positions upon his return. Maynard's company, however, ignored his wife. The vice president of manufacturing knew her and felt she was a "fairly stable type" (which, in fact, she was inside her own culture) and could see no problem. They had no children, which made the selection even easier.

Maynard lasted two months, crashed, was forced to return to the United States, and thoroughly embarrassed his company in its negotiations with this East European country. Why? An analysis revealed that the problem was not Maynard; he loved his work and spent much time on the job. The problem was his wife. She was a right-wing political activist in the United States. Any elementary interviewer could have discovered this and talked it over with her before leaving. As it was, no one did.

Maynard and his wife experienced the normal East European problems for Americans—inability to buy fresh meat and vegetables, inadequate housing by U.S. standards, and the gnawing frustration of living in a totally bureaucratic environment. Rather than enjoying it and attempting to learn, Maynard's wife attacked it politically. The system was wrong and she was right. If someone had explained the environment to Maynard's wife prior to his accepting the position, she might have influenced him to turn it down or he might not have been selected at all.

If a company's domestic system does not involve spouse evaluation, it should at least be considered for international transfers. Outside consultants are a good resource in this area. They can interview the spouse, teenage children (who also may have adjustment problems), and the employee himself. Many employees feel better about doing this outside the company. The consultant can then make both selection and orientation and developmental recommendations on a nonthreatening basis.

Advance Trip

Before a potential expatriate and his spouse can have a meaningful understanding of what it is like to live in a foreign culture, they should at least see the country once. Many multinationals offer expatriate positions without the expatriate ever having seen the host country.

There is a trend toward sending the potential expatriate and his spouse to the country first. Adoption of this trend is definitely recommended. It just is not fair to ask an employee to decide on a foreign assignment with all of its resultant trauma and uprooting of cultural values without his having seen the country. Not that an advance trip of one week will give anyone a thorough understanding of a country's culture, but, if properly done, it will enable the potential expatriate to make a more intelligent decision.

An advance trip should not be a "Yank's tour." The potential expatriate and spouse should be encouraged to go out on their own. One multinational manager makes a potential expatriate on an advance trip find his way back from various remote points in the city, forces the wife to go shopping on her own, and makes the husband order from the menu of a non-English-speaking restaurant.

An expatriate assignment should not be offered until an individual takes an advance trip. If upon return the potential expatriate decides he does not want the assignment, there should be no stigma attached to his declination. If, as in the case of one multinational manager, the potential expatriate is made to feel obligated to accept the position to justify the cost of the advance trip, the purpose is defeated.

Institutionalize the Selection System

A structured selection system is strongly recommended in that it not only serves to achieve consistency but, if properly documented, also communicates the sequence of events necessary to affect an international transfer. In large, culturally diverse multinational companies, a selection system prevents expatriates from being selected for expediency and thus preserves the corporation's philosophy.

Expatriate selection systems should be committed to writing and widely communicated to those involved in the selection system. One example of an expatriate selection tool is an interview worksheet for international candidates (see Table 1). This is a simple device, but quite effective in providing a structured vehicle from which to evaluate international candidates. A potential expatriate should be rated as either satisfactory or unsatisfactory on each of the criteria listed in the table.

Table 1

Interview Worksheet for International Candidates

Motivation
- Investigate reasons and degree of interest in wanting to be considered.
- Determine desire to work abroad, verified by previous concerns such as personal travel, language training, reading, and association with foreign employees or students.
- Determine whether the candidate has a realistic understanding of what working and living abroad requires.
- Determine the basic attitudes of the spouse toward an overseas assignment.

Health
- Determine whether any medical problems of the candidate or his family might be critical to the success of the assignment.
- Determine whether he is in good physical and mental health, without any foreseeable change.

Language Ability
- Determine potential for learning a new language.
- Determine any previous language(s) studied or oral ability (judge against language needed on the overseas assignment).
- Determine the ability of the spouse to meet the language requirements.

Family Considerations
- How many moves has the family made in the past between different cities or parts of the United States?
- What problems were encountered?
- How recent was the last move?
- What is the spouse's goal in this move?
- What are the number of children and the ages of each?
- Has divorce or its potential, death of a family member, etc., weakened family solidarity?
- Will all the children move; why, why not?
- What is the location, health, and living arrangements of grandparents, and the number of trips normally made to their home each year?
- Are there any special adjustment problems that you would expect?

- How is each member of the family reacting to this possible move?
- Do special educational problems exist within the family?

Resourcefulness and Initiative
- Is the candidate independent; can he make and stand by his decisions and judgments?
- Does he have the intellectual capacity to deal with several dimensions simultaneously?
- Is he able to reach objectives and produce results with whatever personnel and facilities he has available, regardless of the limitations and barriers that might arise?
- Can the candidate operate without a clear definition of responsibility and authority on a foreign assignment?
- Will the candidate be able to explain the aims and company philosophy to the local managers and workers?
- Does he possess sufficient self-reliance, self-discipline, and self-confidence to overcome difficulties or handle complex problems?
- Can the candidate work without supervision?
- Can the candidate operate effectively in a foreign environment without normal communications and supporting services?

Adaptability
- Is the candidate sensitive to others, open to the opinions of others, cooperative, and able to compromise?
- What are his reactions to new situations, and efforts to understand and appreciate differences?
- Is he culturally sensitive, aware, and able to relate across the culture?
- Does the candidate understand his own culturally derived values?
- How does the candidate react to criticism?
- What is his understanding of the U.S. government system?
- Will he be able to make and develop contacts with his peers in the foreign country?
- Does he have patience when dealing with problems?
- Is he resilient; can he bounce back after setbacks?

Career Planning
- Does the candidate consider the assignment anything other than a temporary overseas trip?

- Is the move consistent with his progression and that planned by the company?
- Is his career planning realistic?
- What is the candidate's basic attitude toward the company?
- Is there any history or indication of personnel problems with this employee?

Financial
- Are there any current financial and/or legal considerations which might affect the assignment, e.g., house purchase, children and college expenses, car purchases?
- Are financial considerations negative factors, i.e., will undue pressures be brought to bear on the employee or his family as a result of the assignment?

It is also recommended that a system be designed to postpone an expatriate's acceptance of a position until he clearly understands the mechanics of his assignment—how he will be paid, how his taxes will be handled, and what will happen to him when currency relationships change.

Many multinationals are utilizing the "letter of understanding" concept to finalize the selection process. A letter of understanding is a summary of all of the terms and conditions of an international assignment. It serves not only as a communications vehicle but also as a record of the details of an expatriation transaction.

In other countries, employment contracts are utilized to a greater degree than in the United States. An employment contract has a more legal connotation than a letter of understanding. In many U.S. multinationals, letters of understanding serve as declarations of intent as opposed to binding legal agreements. The value of either letters of understanding or employment contracts is that they serve to document and communicate the terms and conditions of international transfers. Their value as a selection tool is that the candidate for an expatriate assignment can see the mechanics of the assignment listed in one specific document. He can look it over one last time before committing himself. Once an employee accepts a letter of understanding, the selection phase is completed and orientation begins.

Bill Revisited

In the first chapter we met Bill, who, as the reader will recall, crashed on a European assignment and was returned to the United States. We shall now examine Bill in light of the expatriation selection guidelines we have explored in this chapter.

As will be recalled, Bill was selected and sent to Brussels because he was the best man in the United States. This was the only selection standard used for Bill. Let us examine what might have happened if he had been selected within a more structured system:

- Bill would first have been interviewed by people who had been there. They would have included returned expatriates who had been assigned to Brussels. If Bill's company could not find anyone who had worked in Brussels, it would have put Bill in contact with sources outside the company and insisted he meet with them. The company would have also had Bill interview a European who could give him an overview of the manner in which business is conducted outside the United States. The results of these discussions would have been a more realistic understanding by Bill of the social and business norms in Europe.

- He and his wife would have been evaluated by an outside consultant. This consultant would not be a part of the company but rather an additional evaluative source. He would have explained to Bill and his wife that the specific results of his tests and interviews would remain confidential but that any potential problem areas would be discussed with both Bill and the company. The results of these tests and interviews would, no doubt, have indicated that Bill's marriage probably could not stand the additional strain of an international assignment. His compulsive nature could make it difficult for him to adjust; and he and his wife may not be the most culturally adaptive candidates for the assignment. This would have been pointed out to Bill and, in a nonspecific way, passed on to the company.

- Assuming that Bill's consideration was not stopped at this point, an advance trip would have been arranged. During this advance trip Bill and his wife would be "turned loose" in Brussels. Situations would have also been arranged such as shopping trips and meals in non-English-speaking restaurants so that they would begin to appreciate both the value of language training and cultural differences. Bill would have also been asked to attend business meetings as an observer in order to give him an appreciation of the business environment.

- Upon return, Bill would have been given candid feedback as to how he was received in Europe, his interpersonal skills, and the necessity for cultural adaptivity. No doubt Bill would either remove himself from consideration or be screened out at this point. If, however, neither of these things happened, he then would have been given a letter of understanding, outlining the terms and conditions of his transfer, and one last chance to refuse the assignment with no stigma attached.

- If Bill had survived to this point, the next step would be that of orientation and training. This is an essential ingredient in any expatriation system and forms the basis for the next chapter.

TO THE EXPATRIATE

Your international assignment may be the best thing that ever happened to you both as a job and as a personal experience. It may also be a disaster. The difference is you—your ability to adapt, your behavioral traits. Do not fool yourself; set your ego aside and evaluate your cultural adaptivity. How do you do this? Start at Chapter 4. Are you a risk taker, an entrepreneur? How about your wife or husband, your children?

Know the country to which you are being sent. If your company will not give you an advance trip, consider paying for one yourself. It is well worth the price if you decide you do not want the assignment.

Use the expatriate worksheet in Chapter 5. It makes an excellent self-evaluation tool. Fill it out on yourself and on all members of your family, and have them do the same. You might also consider having a close friend, someone who knows your family and work habits, fill it out on you.

Most expatriate assignments are either good or bad, very few are neutral. Make sure your experience is positive. If you have doubts, think again before boarding that plane.

Part 4

ORIENTATION AND TRAINING

Chapter 6

ORIENTATION AND TRAINING PRINCIPLES

"He Can't Even Find His Bloody Way in From the Airport"

The scene is the Brussels headquarters of a U.S. multinational. The players are the British expatriate sales manager and the Belgian manager of administration. The problem is the American expatriate technician and family who have just arrived and are waiting at the airport.

"This is the third Yank in a year who has simply shown up and expected to be cared for. Don't they tell them anything!" exclaimed the sales manager.

"Can you imagine just calling from the airport and expecting us to have everything ready at this end?" asked the manager of administration. "We didn't even know he was coming until yesterday. I'll bet he doesn't know anything about the country, how he'll be paid, or how to go about looking for a place to live. We know he can't speak French or Flemish. He's probably got a tourist visa, and no doubt no one in his family has been outside the States before! One of these days we'll have to take a break from baby sitting American expatriates and get some work done!"

"He can't even find his bloody way in from the airport!" interjected the sales manager. "Hope they all fit in my car," he muttered, moving toward the door.

"Here we go again," said the manager of administration, shaking his head while speaking to the just-closed door. "We'll have to spend the first six months getting him organized; he'll be productive for six months; and he'll spend the last six months looking for a job and getting ready to move back."

Each year many versions of this scene are reenacted in the offices of multinational firms throughout the world. The cause is not poor selection or overly sensitive host country management but the lack of an effective expatriate training and orientation program. Even the most culturally adaptive person will run into problems when simply selected, put on an airplane, and expected to cope in his new environment.

The lack of an effective orientation and training program not only causes home and host country management headaches but has serious productivity implications. Why spend a great deal of money to select and transport an expatriate to his new assignment only to have him spend an inordinate amount of time just learning to cope with his new environment? It is much better to train and develop him before he leaves.

The task of home country management does not end with selection; it just begins. There is some very important ground to cover before the expatriate packs his bags. The vehicle for crossing this ground is an orientation and training program. There are, however, some reasons why many multinational firms do not have such a program. The following are some of the more common barriers to setting up a proper orientation and training system:

   Lack of understanding by management—"Why should I invest money to teach Harold, his wife, and three children German? They're only going over there for two years and besides, they speak English at the office anyway."

   Expediency—"Look, this is really an important project. We've got to have Peter over there now. I know it's important that he take cultural training, speak the language, and understand the differences in the way business is conducted, but he'll have to pick that up on his own. We've got to have him there yesterday!"

Structure—"I know we should be doing some kind of training for Lydia before sending her all the way to East Europe, but no one inside my organization can tell me what she should know and I'm no expert on training. I guess I'll just send her and hope she makes it."

Philosophy—"If a man is good enough to be considered for an overseas assignment, he is good enough to work out all of his problems on his own. Why should I send him to any training or spend any more time on him than a domestic transfer?"

The sophisticated multinational employer will overcome these barriers. He will understand the value of a structured orientation program. He will know that selection varies from company to company and from subculture to subculture within a company; and that orientation is extra-organizational and can be objectively done in varying organizational cultures.

Ingredients of an Orientation and Training Program

Companies should have a structured employee orientation and training program. This should not be left to a manager's option, but should be institutionalized in policies, procedures, and practices. The following major phases should be covered.

Phase I: Review of Terms and Conditions of the Assignment

This is the easiest and most inexpensive part of an orientation program, yet one which is overlooked by many employers. It consists of a company representative sitting down with the employee and spouse with the purpose of explaining specific aspects of the assignment. The items covered in this phase of an orientation program should include the following:

- A clear, concise overview of the company's expatriate policies and procedures.

- An explanation of the expatriate compensation system, beginning with a description of its compensation philosophy and progressing into details. Questions should be answered in regard to pay, taxes, and allowances. The expatriate should understand what allowances (expatriate premium, cost of living, swamp pay,* and housing) he will receive and the reasons these are paid.

- Details on the host country location; e.g., details on housing, the local transportation, and the school system.

- A review of moving arrangements. Some of the most mundane details, such as passports, visas, tickets, physical examinations, shipping of household goods, and hotel arrangements, can result in significant problems to the expatriate. It is advisable to review these items during this phase of the orientation.

Our-Company Syndrome

The case of Hilda will illustrate the importance of the spouse's attendance at this phase of the orientation. Prior to her husband's overseas assignment, Hilda had little real interest in his company. She knew what he did and approximately how much he made, but her relationship with the company was remote. She and her husband had many outside activities and did not discuss his company at home.

The relationship changed once Hilda was transferred overseas. The company suddenly assumed a much larger

*For an explanation of swamp pay, see p. 99.

influence on her life. In her mind, it sent her over there, therefore it was responsible for her. A parent–child relationship evolved.

Hilda became dependent on the company's expatriate allowances. She received a housing allowance to help her maintain equivalent housing to that which she had in the United States. A cost-of-living allowance was added to her husband's salary to help her maintain a U.S. standard of living. When the value of the U.S. dollar began to crumble, the company helped her by guaranteeing her purchasing power in local currency units.

She lived in what nationals referred to as the "American ghetto" and what rental agents called the "expatriate community." The majority of the community's population had the same dependency relationship with its employers. As is the case with most dependency relationships, petty jealousies and rivalries arose. These were vented at cocktail parties, where the majority of conversation dealt with salaries, expatriation premiums, home leaves, and company policies. There was a great deal of comparing, and in the tradition of parent–child relationships, a "my dad's bigger than your dad" undercurrent ran through many conversations. In this case the dads were the companies; it was not that one was tougher than another but it was that one company was perceived to have better expatriate benefits than another.

The trouble started when Hilda began to believe that her "dad" really was not as tough as the others. The real cause of Hilda's problem was that she resented the increased dependence she had on the company since she had become an expatriate wife. This resentment of dependence is the root cause of many problems with expatriates, and the sophisticated multinational company will make sure that this subject is discussed before the expatriate transfers. However, Hilda did not go through an orientation program, did not understand her company's basic policies, and had no idea as to its expatriation philosophy. She just did not trust the company and began a negative moral spiral that never ended. One afternoon, in a fit of anger, she wrote an impassioned personal letter to the wife of the company president. By the time she told her husband, it was too late, the letter was on its way across the ocean; he could not do anything about it.

As a result of her letter, Hilda did receive an orientation. A company executive, who was in Europe on other business, spent an evening with Hilda and her husband, explaining the company's expatriate policies and philosophy. The result was that Hilda realized the company was competitive and equitable. It was just that Hilda had been too involved in comparing the parts without understanding the whole. She also did not have a philosophical frame of reference from which to evaluate her company's policies.

It is doubtful if the resentment inherent in the increased dependency relationship can ever be totally removed. However, an orientation program is one way to begin. If Hilda had been given a proper orientation prior to departure, she would have been happier, and the company would have received more return on its investment from her husband. There is a bit of Hilda in all expatriate spouses, and there is a definite tendency for *your* company to become *our* company once an assignment begins.

Phase II: Cultural Training

Once the basics (the company's policies, procedures, and their uses) are covered, cultural training should begin. The purpose of this phase is an understanding of the culture in the host country. In addition to the spouse, this training should include children. If they can walk and talk, they should be included.

Academic and Interpersonal Cultural Training

Cultural training can be approached both through traditional academic techniques or at the interpersonal level.

Academic—There are books, maps, brochures, films, and slides on almost every country in the world. Books can be purchased for expatriates. Slide presentations and films can be shown to the whole family. Local universities can provide instructors for discussions on the history, culture, and socioeconomic patterns of almost any host country.

Interpersonal—There is nothing like being there. As has been indicated, advance trips should be part of the selection process, as should discussions with people who have been there and meetings with national employees now located in the future expatriate's home country. These experiences are also part of orientation and cultural training.

An easy, yet successful technique for a future expatriate wife is an informal luncheon with a wife who has recently returned from an assignment in the future host country. The topics can range from social amenities to how one buys meat at the local butcher shops.

The techniques and amount of interpersonal cultural training vary both with the expatriate and the country of assignment. Obviously, a U.S. expatriate sent to an English-speaking Commonwealth country would require less cultural training than an American sent to a non-English-speaking underdeveloped country.

A new form of interpersonal training is emerging. Its technology is borrowed from organizational development efforts, and many of its tools are taken from the laboratory training techniques of the behavioral scientist. It is possible to expose the future expatriate to training sessions on relating authentically to people in different cultures, the value of candor and interpersonal feedback in cross-cultural communications, nonverbal communications, and how to understand what your foreign counterpart is really saying.

The opportunities for the potential expatriate to take this type of training are becoming more widespread. The value of this kind of interpersonal training should increase when the right combination of interdisciplinary resources becomes more crystallized and more sources are made available.

Phase III: Language Training

If the ingredients necessary for a successful expatriate assignment, both on and off the job, were reduced to just one option, it would clearly be a knowledge of the language. It is possible to go through an expatriate assignment without learning the host country language. Many companies do not require it; others feel it is of dubious value in an expatriate's performance. They are wrong! It is the most important thing they can give an expatriate to assure a successful assignment.

If you know the host country language, you will have a key to its culture. You will understand its subtleties and will be a better expatriate in an infinite number of ways. The importance of learning the language cannot be overemphasized. You just miss too much without it!

There is no easy way to learn a language. There are a number of techniques ranging from formal classroom instruction to cassette recorders and telephone contact with an instructor. There is no ideal way. The only common ingredient in learning a language is motivation and understanding of its value for the assignment. Learning a language takes time and work, but it is well worth the effort.

A company cannot make its expatriates learn a language. It can, however, positively reinforce the value of language training. Since learning a language requires discipline, dedication, and time, commodities some expatriates are short of when preparing to go overseas, it is important that managers concerned with multinational people movement adopt a firm, but evangelical, approach to the necessity for language training.

Negative Rationales

In order to reinforce the value of language training, one must be able to deal with the common reasons expatriates do not think it is necessary. The following are the major rationales potential expatriates utilize when discussing language training:

Not enough time—"I've got to be on the job in three months. Before then, I've got to wrap up what I'm doing back here. There's no way I can take language training."

There are two mistakes here: (a) Companies send expatriates overseas for periods of years and should allow them sufficient time to learn the language before leaving. Anything less is simply management for expediency and not results. Any international manpower-planning system that cannot give an expatriate adequate time to learn at least the basics of the language just is not working. (b) The other half of the problem is, of course, the expatriate himself. He has to make time to learn the language. Learning the language of the host country is the most important thing he can do to get ready for a foreign assignment.

I will take it over there—"It will be easier for me to take the language when I get overseas. Everyone else there will speak it and I'll be motivated to learn the language."

This will not work. Chances are that he will not do it. If the expatriate is an American, he will usually be able to converse on a business level in English (if he is not an American, chances are he knows the language anyway). The track record of expatriates in learning the language after arrival in the host country is poor. There are just too many other things to worry about. The expatriate is starting a number of things from scratch—a new house, a new job, a new life style—and will not start to learn a new language at the same time. Many make futile tries, usually after they have been in the country for six months or so, but very few succeed. They have already been conditioned toward a tourist existence.

It is much better to take the basics of a language before leaving; that way it is more familiar. It is hard enough for an expatriate to force himself to use his new skills once he gets over there. It is very difficult for him to pick up the rudimentary skills as well.

No need to learn the language—"I don't need it; they all speak English. I've got better things to do than to learn a language at my age."

Foolish! Foolish! Foolish! The reader by now knows a number of rebuttals to this commonly expressed concern.

Unable to learn languages—"I can't learn a language. I took two years in college and barely passed. There is no sense in investing all that money to send me to language school. I'll just botch it anyway."

This is nonsense. While it is true that some people have a better aptitude for learning languages than others, anyone smart enough to be in a position where a company is willing to invest thousands of dollars to send him on an overseas assignment has the ability to learn a language. It may take some longer than others, but motivation is a great equalizer in linguistic ability.

Just me—"Okay, I understand that I should take language training, but I don't want to subject my family to hours of study. They have enough to do before moving overseas. I'll take it and, when we get there, I'll do most of the talking."

A knowledge of the language is perhaps of more value to the family than to the expatriate. The family has to cope with a different environment—attend schools, go shopping, and live outside the insulation of a multinational English-speaking office building.

Methods of Language Training

There is no ideal method to teach an expatriate a language. The following are the common methods used by most multinational companies.

Individual instruction at a language school—There are specialized language schools with offices in most large cities of the United States. Some have offices throughout the world. These schools utilize various techniques, such as cassette recordings, face-to-face instruction, and programmed learning. Employers doing a great deal of language training generally buy blocks of time from these schools. The advantages of these schools are that they are flexible in their scheduling, thus accommodating a busy expatriate and his family, and are usually of good quality.

Intensive programs—Language schools, universities, and companies themselves have planned intensive periods of linguistic training. The basic technique is to involve the student in the language intensively over a specific span of time. For example, these sessions may be held for one week in a motel. The student must speak only the foreign language for the entire time—ordering all meals, reading all papers, and conversing only in the new language. Another variation is attending a school for eight hours a day and only using the language. The advantages of this intensive training are that it may be done at once and will be all the expatriate has to think about during the training period. An additional advantage is to have the expatriate relocate immediately at the conclusion of the training period. This helps promote carry over to his host country.

Do-it-yourself kits—There are a number of variations: records, cassette recordings, books, telephone conversations with instructors, and combinations of these techniques. The main advantage of do-it-yourself kits is time. The future expatriate and his family may proceed at their own pace in the home or office. This form of language training should be used as a complement to other forms, unless one has an extremely motivated expatriate. The reality of do-it-yourself language training is that without the friendly prodding of an instructor, most potential expatriates just do not get very far.

Formal classroom training—This is a more traditional approach to learning a language and involves an instructor and a roomfull of students. This form of training, while effective, is inflexible for the student who wants individual attention and must take a number of lessons in a short period of time.

Regardless of the technique, the one central ingredient in learning a language is motivation on the part of the student. It is incumbent upon the multinational employer to emphasize the need for language training.

This chapter has offered an overview of the ingredients of an expatriate orientation and training program. In the next chapter, we will journey through an orientation program with an expatriate family and, thus, have the opportunity to see these principles reflected in a specific situation.

Chapter 7

ORVILLE'S ORIENTATION

This chapter offers both a practical illustration of the principles of orientation and training, and a concluding discussion of in-house versus outside and re-entry programs. We will begin with Orville.

Orville has been selected to be the project manager of a new venture in East Europe. This venture is the joint management of an electronics manufacturing operation between Orville's firm and the country's ministry of electronics. He is expected not only to work well with local nationals but also to account for his company's interest in the project. The expected duration of his assignment is four years, at which time he will be replaced by a national.

Orville and his family are flown to the corporate headquarters. Orville's company processes a number of expatriates so that it has a central personnel function dedicated to the people aspects of international business. The first morning Orville and his wife meet with a representative to discuss his letter of understanding. Orville has two teenage children who could attend this session; however, Orville has requested that they do not (this usually depends on the degree that family financial resources are communicated to children and varies from expatriate to expatriate).

The morning begins with a cassette slide presentation of the company's expatriation policies. Standard items, such as home leave provisions, expatriate salary adders, expatriate premium, cost-of-living allowance, shelter allowance, remote site premium, and educational provisions, are covered.

Orville and his wife have traveled overseas and thus have passports, but the children do not, and the company helps with the applications. The company also begins the process of helping secure the proper visas and work permit. (It is amazing how many expatriates arrive in their host countries with the wrong visas. This not only starts the assignment out on the wrong foot but does not promote good will with either the host country organization or the government. An effort by the company to make sure that the right visas are secured before the expatriate leaves can alleviate these problems.)

The next step is an in-depth coverage of Orville's letter of understanding. It proceeds slowly; Orville gets fidgety, but the personnel representative knows the value of going through it. It is intended that Orville understand the agreement and that his wife receive a vaccination against too bad a case of "our-company syndrome."

It is now lunch time. Orville, his wife, and children are taken to lunch by a recently returned expatriate and his wife. Unfortunately, Orville's company has had no one in this particular East European country, but this couple was located in Vienna and he was required to travel widely in East Europe during his assignment.

Upon returning from lunch, Orville and his family are put in a conference room. A professor from the local university who teaches, among other things, East European history joins them. (This is an inexpensive and effective device as it only costs the company a half day's consulting fee.) The afternoon is spent in a discussion of the history, culture, and economics of Orville's future host country. The family is given books, maps, and even some tourist brochures describing its new country.

Orville and his wife spend most of the next morning with a representative of the payroll department. The subject is how Orville will be paid and an explanation of the company's tax policy. They leave the meeting understanding how Orville will be paid and in what currency. (This is a rather complicated transaction, because part of Orville's salary will be paid to him in the currency of the host country from the joint venture company. Since this is "soft" currency, not convertible outside the country, and Orville elects to have part of his salary deposited in a U.S. bank, the "how" of his salary payment is important for both he and the company to understand.) They also understand the company's tax equalization policy. (The company will withhold a tax that approximates that which Orville would have paid if he had remained in the United States. The company will then pay all non-U.S. taxes.) Orville's specific "hypothetical" tax will be decided at a later meeting, but he and his wife now understand the company's tax philosophy.

Orville and his wife then have a brief review of the expatriation provisions with the personnel representative, questions from the day before are answered, and Orville's future boss joins them for lunch. The subjects are language and cultural training.

Orville has been given sufficient lead time. He will not be relocating for nine months. A national language school is located in Orville's current city of assignment. This school has a trained instructor in the new language. A program is arranged whereby Orville, his wife, and two children will each take a minimum of 200 hours of the language before departing. This is agreed to by Orville and his boss. (It, in fact, becomes an objective against which Orville will be measured.)

Because of the cultural differences in this East European country, a program is planned with a consulting firm specializing in cultural orientation. The consulting firm, in turn, has access to a number of university resources. A one-week intensive course is arranged for Orville and his family. This course covers: (a) culturally derived values of his future host country; (b) social, economic, and political institutions;

(c) how business is transacted; and (d) "do's and don'ts" in social life.

Orville's two children are in high school. It was his original intention to have them attend school in his host country; however, it was soon apparent that there were no equivalent schools in this country and he decided that they will remain in the United States, stay with relatives, and attend school. They will, however, spend summers and vacations in the host country. The company's policy on how much of the children's travel expenses it will pay is discussed and understood—one of the purposes of an orientation program is to avoid surprises.

When Orville and his family return home from their visit to company headquarters, they have a structured program for orientation and training prior to their relocation. Language training is emphasized and becomes a part of Orville's work objectives before he leaves. Most potential surprises have been discussed. For example, Orville knows the degree of support the company will give him in transporting his children during summer vacations. Far better to know before you leave than to be surprised when an expense voucher is returned while overseas.

Orville and his family will still have a number of adjustments to make upon arrival, but they are far better prepared than the expatriate who is simply put on an airplane and expected to cope. Because of his understanding of culturally derived value systems, Orville will be effective more quickly on the job.

Front-End Versus Rear-End Programs

This section has emphasized front-end orientation and training programs—those that happen before an expatriate relocates to his host country. There are some companies that also provide rear-end programs, or programs that happen once the expatriate has relocated to the host country.

It is recommended that the bulk of orientation and training be done before relocation. Once an expatriate relocates, he is caught in ongoing learning situations. The expatriate must cope on the job; the children must enter educational institutions; and the wife must maintain a household. They are generally too busy to formally learn.

Rear-end orientation is, however, useful. It must complement and be subservient to front-end training and is usually most effective when related to specific problems such as housing or schools.

In-House Versus Outside Training

In-house training and orientation, that done by the company itself, is very useful because the company can link its own policies and procedures into a training and orientation program. However, many companies do not have the internal resources to provide an effective program.

Outside programs, those provided by universities and consulting firms, can be useful also. There are a number of effective resources which can be purchased to help in an orientation program. These are most needed when an expatriate is going to a hard country, or if a company does not have a large number of expatriates and cannot justify an in-house program.

In many cases, a combination of both is most effective. An example of this was illustrated in the case of Orville. The in-house portion emphasized the company's policies, procedures, and some cultural training; the outside portion utilized resources unavailable internally.

Reentry Orientation

If a company has an effective manpower-planning system and the expatriate is kept in cultural contact with his home country through home leaves, internal communications, and compensation practices, the need for reentry orientation is minimized. However, even in these cases, some type of counseling and reorientation is useful. The techniques vary according to the company's structure. The following items should be examined:

- Changes in the company's organizational structure since the expatriate left.

- The expatriate's new job and how it fits into the structure.

- Changes in living patterns, housing, and transportation systems since he left. (That is if the expatriate returns to the same city; if not, an overview of the subject for his new location should be given. Many expatriates remember only the good things and then only as they were before they left. When surprised with increases in the cost of living, particularly housing and food, while losing their expatriate premiums, they enter into agonizing waves of reverse cultural shock.)

- A review of the repatriation provisions, i.e., what is paid for and what allowances are granted.

- Counseling to help fend off the big-fish-in-small-pond syndrome.

The more effective the manpower-planning and communication system, the less important becomes reentry orientation. However, based on current practices of many multinationals, reentry orientation still needs to be built into an international people management system.

Proper Orientation Equals Adult/Adult–Company/Employee Relationship

A proper orientation and training system is often the key ingredient to a successful overseas assignment. With one, an expatriate is prepared to cope, knows what to expect, and goes into a foreign assignment in an adult/adult relationship with his company. Without one, a parent/child relationship often develops and an assignment can turn sour.

There is no area where an adult/adult relationship is more important than in the area of compensation. When an expatriate and a company discuss base salary, taxes, benefits, and allowances, it is most helpful if an atmosphere of mutual trust and candor exists. The subject of compensation in an international environment is covered in the next chapter.

TO THE EXPATRIATE

Do not just put your family on that airplane and expect to cope automatically when you land. It is a whole different world when you get off the plane on the other side of that border. You had better do all you can to get yourself and your family ready before you go. You will be too busy trying to adjust when you arrive to worry about any kind of training.

Learn about the people, the history, the culture of your host country. It will help you on the job and make your off-the-job experiences rich and educational. If you can walk into your foreign office and utter only one simple sentence in the language, you will be far above the average U.S. expatriate. If you are even semifluent in the language of your host country and understand the basics of its culture and value system, you will not only astound and win the admiration of your local business associates but also practically guarantee a successful assignment. You will also take off the blinders many expatriates wear and begin to appreciate that whole rich, interesting, historical world that exists outside those insulated multinational walls of your office, and move beyond the barrier of exported U.S. cultural values that surrounds the American ghetto.

Read Chapter 6 again. Your company has the obligation to make you more effective—after all it is spending thousands of dollars to send you to another country. You have the right to expect it to maximize its investment. If your company wants to send you without training, there is something wrong. Let your boss read this book; show it to your personnel manager. If they still show no interest in training, you may either reevaluate the assignment or begin training yourself.

The following are five simple steps you can do on your own:

- Make sure the basics are covered—Chapter 6 gives an overview under "Phase I: Orientation and Training."

- Try the public library—You may be able to find films, records, and slides; at the very least you will find books.

- Try your local university or college—There may be existing cross-cultural programs. You may be lucky; you might run into a student or faculty member from your future host country.

- Look within your own company—There may be returned expatriates, non-U.S. expatriates who may be assigned to your operation, or recently returned business travelers within your company.

- Learn the language—It is the most important thing you can do before you go. Read all the reasons why expatriates think they do not need it in Chapter 6, then learn it. If your company will not pay for it, take it yourself; it will be the best investment you can make to assure a successful assignment.

Part 5

COMPENSATION BASICS

Chapter 8

CULTURAL COMPENSATION

The final evaluation of any compensation system is in its perceived value. Since people are a product of their cultures, and values are culturally derived, what is perceived as positive by one person may be perceived as negative by another. The perceived value of monetary compensation, for example, varies within a country. Money may be very important to the striving middle manager in the Midwest and of little concern to the artist in California.

Since there are variations in value systems within one country, what happens when one must, as in the case of multinational compensation decisions, expand the consideration to more than one country? What tends to happen is confusion, unless one has an appreciation of cultural compensation.

Exportation of Cultural Compensation

Historically, multinationals have attempted to export the cultural compensation values of their headquarters country. The exporting of the cultural compensation values of the headquarters country usually creates problems, as illustrated in the example of the Asian administrator.

87

The Asian Administrator

"I can't believe he quit!" exclaimed the U.S.-based manager to his personnel vice president after being suddenly notified that his Asian director of administration had resigned. "I paid him at least 40 percent more than anyone in a similar position makes in that country."

Upon examination, it became clear that the problem was the U.S. manager's cultural compensation blindness. Base salary meant more in the United States than in the country in which his Asian administrator was located. The reason the person quit had to do with his cultural compensation value index which was based on different criteria than that of his U.S. boss. True, the Asian administrator was given a big salary, but the problem was that his index was based on status rather than money. The real reason he left was the size and physical appearance of his office. It was small, shoddy, and located in an old building. His office caused him to lose "face" and doubling his salary would not have helped. Less salary and a modern office would have done wonders and certainly cost the company less.

Another example of cultural compensation blindness is the wholesale exportation of compensation systems that emphasize incentives, bonuses, and commissions by U.S. marketing organizations. The underlying philosophy is, of course, that money motivates. The proof of this is inadequate within the United States. In other cultures it is even more suspect. In many countries psychological factors appear to have more to do with motivation than with salary. The sophisticated multinational employer must guard against the cultural compensation bias of the headquarters country and be aware of the psychological aspects of compensation. When, therefore, a compensation system is designed for a country, like many in Asia, with a highly stratified society where perquisites and status vary radically by social level, it must be realized that things like a private parking space, the size of an office, or the assignment of a private secretary, even when one is not really needed, may be of more value in terms of cultural compensation than U.S.-based incentive schemes.

Salary, Benefits, and Tax Relationship

On the nonpsychological level, the relationship among salary, benefits, and taxes varies by country. There are high-salary/low-tax countries, low-salary/high-tax countries, and some where income taxes are high, but it is culturally acceptable not to pay them or to cheat.

The example of Trevor, the reluctant Englishman in Chapter 2, illustrates this relationship and its critical importance to the multinational employer. Trevor's case, and that of most Englishmen working outside the United Kingdom, illustrates the importance of an established system for dealing with the relationship between salary and taxes. In terms of this relationship, the world can roughly be divided into two categories as follows: *high-salary/low-tax countries*—the prime example is the United States; and *high-tax/low-salary countries*—an example of a country falling into this category is the United Kingdom. Without a system, transfers between these two categories become hopelessly snarled.

The salary, benefits, and tax relationship varies by culture. The psychological aspects of compensation also are dependent on the setting of one's cultural compensation index. What, then, happens when a person moves from one system to another? What is the result of culturally derived value systems on expatriate compensation?

The result has been confusion, counterproductivity, and administrative chaos to all but those firms which have clear expatriation philosophies and support them with a structuralist approach. Nowhere is it more important to have clear definition, uniform philosophy, and consistent administration than in expatriate compensation. On a narrow level, the lack of a systematic approach to international compensation will result in badly motivated expatriates, confused local national organizations, and headquarters managers devoting an inordinate amount of time to the unsnarling of international compensation problems. On a broad level, it results in a serious depletion of the effectiveness of a company's international human resources. The problems inherent in the lack of a clear system or the discipline to follow a philosophy can be illustrated in the following examples.

Three Men in Paris

The company, an international electronics conglomerate, has three expatriates in its Paris office. All three are department managers with basically the same position, yet all three are treated differently.

Peter, an American, traveled to France while a student, returned to the United States and married after his career was established with the firm. On impulse, he asked to be transferred to Paris. The manager of the French subsidiary liked Peter's background, but could not afford the financial commitment necessary to bring Peter over as an expatriate; therefore, Peter was hired as a "local national." This meant that he received limited assistance on relocation, but no expatriation allowances or language training for his wife. Peter was paid and taxed as though he were a Frenchman.

Paul, who had the office next to Peter, was a full-fledged U.S. expatriate. He had participated in language and cultural training, was paid a U.S. salary, with taxes equalized to a U.S. level, received a housing allowance enabling him to live in an excellent section of the city, received an expatriation premium for living overseas, and was paid a monthly cost-of-living allowance, theoretically enabling him to buy goods and services as though he were in the United States. His children were able to go to the best schools through the company's educational allowance. He also received an expatriate's annual home leave and topped off his compensation package with currency protection against the devaluation of the U.S. dollar in its relation to the French franc. Paul was no more or less an American than Peter.

Earl was a Frenchman who had spent three years in the United States and was then sent to Brussels as a U.S. expatriate (the company had no other policy). He then was transferred back to Paris, not as a Frenchman (because he refused to go in that status and was too valuable not to send) but as a U.S. expatriate with the same benefits as Paul. His office was located across the hall.

One day the three of them and their boss, a French national, had lunch. After the third bottle of wine, things came to a head. Peter was incensed over Paul's expatriate premiums. Paul could afford to go out at night and enjoy the advantages of living in Paris. He drove a new car and his wife was active in the expatriate community. Peter, however, could barely afford to buy food (living as a Frenchman was not as easy as he thought). His wife, who could not speak the language, was an increasing burden to him. Since he had relinquished any right to be repatriated (the company thought of him as a Frenchman), he could see no way out. He was thoroughly broke, depressed, and jealous of a peer who was existing in a totally different socioeconomic stratum.

Earl was much better off than his boss in that he was classified as a U.S. expatriate. His boss had a difficult time understanding why a Frenchman returning to France should be treated like an American. Four bottles of wine later, the head office received a telephone call, a personnel representative was dispatched, and the situation was eventually unsnarled. A postmortem of this situation reveals the following general principles which can easily be applied to other companies: (a) Americans transferring as local nationals usually do not work out; (b) local nationals returning to their home country as expatriates do not work out any better; and (c) a clear, consistent philosophy on compensation of employees transferring across borders is always needed.

The Company Car That Broke the Camel's Back

Harold was a U.S. expatriate manufacturing manager sent to a large manufacturing facility in suburban London. Harold came to the United Kingdom complete with a full package of expatriation incentives, including a cost-of-living allowance, an expatriation premium, U.S. salary and taxes, and a housing allowance. Although Harold was single, he still proceeded to rent a very expensive house (one which none of the local managers could have afforded) and began to live the life that only a single swinger can live in London.

Harold's ostentatious life style soon raised the ire of his British peers. They took their complaints to their plant manager, who gave them the party line. "Our company has a very sophisticated expatriation system. Its purpose is to allow people transferring from one country to another to live the same sort of life that they would have lived in their home country. To that end, Harold has a housing allowance because housing is more expensive here than the U.S., and in order to stay the same, he needs to receive this allowance. The same holds true for his cost-of-living allowance. It just costs more to live as an American here. His expatriation premium is something we give all expatriate employees in order to help them cope with a different environment. All in all, Harold is simply utilizing these allowances for their purpose in helping him to live as though he hadn't left the U.S."

His colleagues grudgingly accepted this—at least until the company car. Most Commonwealth countries have relatively high taxes, and executives receive perquisites. Many of these are designed to give compensation in a nontaxable manner. Harold's peers all had company automobiles. It was part of the cultural compensation system. Harold's boss in the United States did not think twice about approving Harold's requisition for a company car. After all, he was in the United Kingdom and they all had company cars over there. Right? Wrong! When Harold received the company car, it blew the whole expatriation rationale. If the purpose of the expatriation premiums was to help treat Harold the same as though he were in the United States, he would, therefore, receive a company car only if the company would have given him one in the United States—it would not have. Harold was taking advantage of a culturally derived compensation practice. His company's expatriation philosophy was to let him take advantage of culturally derived compensation practices of his home country, not that of his host country. The local nationals, who grudgingly accepted the plant manager's earlier rationale, raised such a furror that Harold not only lost his company car but also was transferred back to the United States. Compensation practices need to be consistent with philosophy. It is essential that expatriate compensation respond to this dictate.

Wolfgang's Rebellion

Wolfgang was manager of his firm's research and development (R&D) operations in Germany. In that capacity he had administratively supervised a string of three U.S. expatriate engineers over the past six years. Wolfgang was slated to eventually assume a higher management position. "Wouldn't it be nice to bring Wolfgang to the U.S. for a couple of years, get him acclimated to the corporate way of doing things, and then send him back to Germany?" said the U.S. vice president of R&D. Soon, Wolfgang was bound for the United States.

A U.S. expatriate going to Germany in Wolfgang's company would receive U.S. benefits, pay U.S. taxes, and receive an expatriation premium, a cost-of-living allowance, a housing allowance, and currency protection. However, when a non-U.S. employee came to the United States, Wolfgang's company simply paid him a U.S. salary, expected him to pay U.S. taxes, and forgot about him. (This is typical of many U.S.-controlled multinationals.) Wolfgang, however, reflected the new prosperity and increasing independence of many European subsidiaries. He rebelled, wanting the same incentives as his U.S. friends received while in Germany. He wanted a German cost-of-living allowance while in the United States, a housing allowance, company reimbursement of his contribution toward Social Security taxes ("what good will it do me as a German; I'm not going to retire here"), company maintenance of German benefit levels, and, of course, he wanted to take his German holidays ("after all the Americans took the Fourth of July when in Germany") and his German vacation (longer than that of his U.S. peers). Wolfgang, in fact, wanted equality—to be treated the same as the U.S. expatriates had been treated in Germany.

Wolfgang lost the battle but won the war for future expatriates. He was promptly sent back to Germany, but the company eventually did reevaluate its expatriate compensation system and moved toward equality.

The Third-Country National

Then, of course, there is the third-country national whose proper compensation is sometimes bewildering, even in the best structured situations. The example of Pierre in the first chapter will serve to illustrate this point.

Man Without a Country

Another, more long-range problem is illustrated by Ian; the retirement problems of "soldier of fortune" type employees.

Ian, originally from Sydney, took his first job with an American multinational, which sent him to New Guinea as part of its mining operations. This particular company did business in many countries, but did not have a career expatriation program; rather it sent expatriates on relatively short-term assignments and returned them to their home countries. Ian represented the small minority of employees who liked living outside their home country and who more or less continued permanently on expatriation assignments.

While in New Guinea, Ian participated in the company's Australian superannuation program. However, he was next sent to South Africa, resigning from the company's Australian subsidiary and accumulating credits in the South African's subsidiary retirement plan. From South Africa, Ian was sent to the company's administrative offices in London, resigning from the South African subsidiary. From London Ian was sent to the United States and from the United States to Brazil.

Ian, now in his mid 50s, literally finds himself a man without a country. He has accumulated small pieces of individual country retirement plans, none of which will help him a great deal when he retires. Since he works for a company that does not have offshore benefits for career expatriates, Ian is now in a bind.

There are soldiers of fortune in many multinational companies, many of whom do not worry about retirement or even a final country until it is too late in their careers. It is the task of an effective expatriate compensation system to respond to the needs of the Ians of the world, help define a country of origin, and have the systems capability to respond to their problems.

This chapter has dealt with the cultural background of international compensation. In order to structure a rational compensation system, it is also necessary to have an appreciation for the terminology of multinational compensation. This is the task of the next chapter.

Chapter 9

TERMINOLOGY

If one were to stand unobserved in the corner of a convention of international compensation experts, one would be exposed to a number of terms. The terms such as "expatriation premium" or "cost-of-living allowance" would become the subject of prolonged discussions. The uninitiated might conclude that there is a common understanding of these terms. This, unfortunately, is not the case.

It is important to have a general understanding of these terms in order to discuss an expatriate compensation system. Therefore, it is the purpose of this chapter not only to provide an overview of the common expatriate terms but also to provide some insight into their utilization.

Expatriation Premium

This is generally expressed as a percentage of base salary (ranging from 5 to 30 percent or more). It is paid tax free in some companies, while it is taxed in others. Its purpose also varies. In companies taking a modular approach to expatriation compensation, it is a combination of compensation for living away from a home country and an inducement to take an overseas assignment. In this case the percentage is usually low. In other firms, primarily those taking a nonmodular approach and bundling all allowances together, it is intended that the expatriation premium compensate for all overseas problems, and it is therefore higher.

An early example of the expatriation premium was the British government's overseas allowance system. Just as the British Empire has declined, so has the popularity of the expatriation premium among many multinationals. Its validity is suspect with the increasing trend toward unbundling expatriation compensation. Unbundling refers to the concept of having a specific purpose for each module of expatriation compensation, such as a cost-of-living allowance, to offset differences in living costs, and a housing allowance to pay for housing differences. In an unbundled system, each of these modules is shown separately. Thus, there is concern over the necessity of an expatriation premium.

The need for expatriation premiums in an unbundled environment becomes a matter of a company's assumptions on motivation. Is it necessary to pay a premium to attract and motivate an employee for an overseas assignment? Perhaps this was so in the heyday of the British Empire, but many multinationals are becoming dubious in today's unbundled world.

Cost-of-Living Allowance

The concept of paying cost-of-living allowances is heavily utilized by U.S. multinationals. Cost-of-living allowances vary, as they can be unbundled or bundled (some include housing, others do not; some include remote site and hardship allowances, others do not). The purpose of a cost-of-living allowance, however, is basically to provide for the difference in living costs between the home country and the host country.

Many U.S. multinationals receive data from the cost-of-living index prepared by the State Department. This compares a "market basket" of goods and services from non-

U.S. locations to the cost of similar goods and services in the United States. This index, then, may be expressed as a percentage of an employee's base salary. Since the U.S. dollar is used as a base for purchasing power in these market-basket studies, its strength against local currency units also has much to do with the use of the index. Many increases in cost-of-living allowances have as much to do with currency realignments as with the cost of goods and services.

Cost-of-living indexes range from zero (most companies do not have negative indexes) to over 50 percent. The majority of companies do not apply this index to an expatriate's gross salary. Some (those that split income) apply the index to only the portion paid in the host country. Others make assumptions as to how much of a person's income is spent in a foreign location and apply the index to that amount. One formula, for example, utilizes the State Department index, adjusts it to the current exchange rate, and applies it to 60 percent of an expatriate's base salary with a maximum of $2,500 per month to which it is applied.

There are also consultants in the business of supplying spendable income curves and selling cost-of-living data. Such a firm will provide, for any desired geographic location, an estimate of the amount of money an expatriate can be expected to spend on cost-of-living items. This estimate can be broken down both by salary level and by family size. Some of these firms take their own surveys; others utilize sources such as the State Department index. All are similar in that they end up giving the company an estimate of the amount of money that should be granted to an expatriate, depending on his family size, income, and geographic location.

The advantage of purchasing spendable income curves and cost-of-living data is that a company can simply add to an expatriate's salary whatever amount of money the consultant indicates is necessary. The disadvantage is, of course, that many companies have only a vague idea how the firm arrived at the amount and, therefore, cannot explain it in full to an expatriate.

Cost-of-living allowances are generally U.S. geocentric, i.e., they are given to U.S. expatriates but not to foreign nationals in the United States. Some companies have experimented with cost-of-living allowances for third-country nationals. However, the lack of reliable data has tended to cause more problems than solutions.

Swamp Pay Allowance

Swamp pay can be broken down into two areas: remote site and hazardous duty. These terms are used interchangeably in many companies. In some unbundled systems they are broken out with remote site as a percentage adder to base pay for living in areas of cultural deprivation, i.e., no schools, transportation, and/or entertainment. Hazardous duty areas are those where a physical danger is present, such as war zones. In reality, remote sites are often hazardous duty and very few expatriates go to areas of actual combat. These allowances are really forms of expatriation premiums and basically have the purpose of paying for a disutility. As the world becomes more sophisticated, with the exception of remote mining and other natural resource development areas, there are fewer and fewer needs for swamp pay.

Shelter Allowance

Adequate housing is culturally derived and, therefore, varies from country to country. Until recently, most housing allowances have been U.S. geocentric—Americans have relatively large houses and pay a relatively small portion of their salaries for them. Recently housing allowances have increasingly been utilized for expatriates coming into the United States as well as other non-U.S. expatriates. The following are the common types of housing allowances.

Flat Amount

Just as cost-of-living data can be purchased so can housing data. For a fee, the multinational employer can get a list of countries and the amount of money the company should contribute to an expatriate's housing. There are also consulting firms, which are located in many international cities, that assist expatriates in securing proper housing.

The flat allowance has the advantage of simplicity. An expatriate can be told that he will get a certain amount each month to help defray housing costs. It also has the advantage of responding to areas such as Japan and Hong Kong, where housing is very expensive relative to U.S. costs and standards.

Formula

A formula approach is a method of sharing housing costs between the expatriate and the employer. An example of this is the 10/80/20 housing formula. This assumes that an expatriate would pay 10 percent of his base salary toward housing, the company would then pay 80 percent of the remainder, and the expatriate would pay the top 20 percent. Assuming an expatriate's base salary is $1,000 per month and the house he rents costs $300 per month, the 10/80/20-percent formula works as follows:

1. Initial employee payment = 10% of base salary = $100;
2. Balance of rent = $300 − $100 = $200;
3. Company share = 80% of balance of rent = $160;
4. Remainder owed by employee = 20% of balance of rent = $40;
5. Total = $100 + $160 + $40 = $300.

The formula approach has the advantage of allowing the expatriate more flexibility and giving him the opportunity to participate in the choice of his housing style and location. One disadvantage is the "Castle on the Rhine" approach, whereby the expatriate with modest housing in the United

States rents a huge palace and the company is not only embarrassed by his choice but also spending more money than is necessary. In high-expense areas such as Japan, formula housing also has the disadvantage of forcing the expatriate to pay a disproportionate amount relative to what he would have paid for equivalent housing in his home country. Most formula equations work well if local management has the authority to review the appropriateness and cost of housing.

Company-Owned Housing

Some companies own their own residences. Expatriates simply move into them at either no cost or a predetermined amount. This approach works well in remote sites where no housing is available, in areas where housing is very expensive (and where it is less expensive for tax reasons for a company to own its own housing), and in companies where there are very few expatriates and the house becomes an "embassy" to the business community in terms of prestige and status.

The advantage of company-owned housing is ease and flexibility. The major disadvantage is that companies using a balance sheet approach must charge the expatriate for housing which is not of his own choice.

Educational Allowance

This is a U.S. geocentric allowance. In the United States the majority of families, regardless of socioeconomic status, send their children to public schools. When transferring overseas, it is sometimes impossible to find adequate public schools, and the expatriate must find private schools. Educational allowances are granted to pay for schools, uniforms, and other educational expenses that would not have been encountered if they had remained in the United States.

The administration of educational allowances varies from organization to organization. Most pay the actual tuition for schools; some pay for transportation, uniforms, and other expenses. For expatriates assigned in countries where there are no schools, companies usually pay tuition in either boarding schools or transportation expenses to and from the home country to visit students who have remained behind.

Educational standards and methods are also culturally derived. The use of educational allowances has expanded and now includes expatriates to the United States and non-U.S. expatriates. Many companies are paying for correspondence lessons to keep students in proper progression in their home country schools, so that when they return they are able to continue without having to repeat any missed levels or course sequences.

Home Leave

Home leaves are granted to many expatriates. It is generally agreed that the purpose of home leaves is to reacquaint expatriates with living patterns in their home countries, allow them to conduct business that must be done first hand, and allow them to visit relatives and friends. Home leave practices have deviated from these purposes. In some multinationals, one finds expatriates touring foreign countries while on home leave. This not only defeats the purpose but also irritates local nationals, who perceive this as another vacation. In other multinationals, it is a practice to "buy" home leaves. If an expatriate is needed on assignment during the time he is expected to take home leave, the company may choose to pay him for not taking it. This, again, defeats the purpose. Home leaves should not be geocentric. Most companies find the same need for cultural reacquaintance to the home country for all types of expatriates.

Other Allowances

There are, naturally, a host of other allowances ranging from clothing allowances, when moving people from tropical to continental climates, to providing chauffeur-driven company cars. It has not been the intent of the above definitions to provide an exhaustive survey of all overseas allowances, but rather to provide an overview of the common terms, and set the stage for the next chapter in which a systems approach will be discussed.

TO THE EXPATRIATE

You are a creature of your culture. Your compensation is just one of a number of culturally derived values. It, however, is one that you bring with you on an overseas assignment. Your company should be able to relate your compensation to your culture. If you are an American, you should be compensated as an American no matter where you are located. Beware of going overseas under a "special" less-than-American status. No special deal is worth throwing away your culturally derived value system. Remember our friends from Paris in Chapter 8—do not get trapped.

Be content with your cultural compensation; do not be greedy, it will only get you in trouble as it did to Harold in Chapter 8.

If you are a career expatriate in a company where there is no international division, or no offshore benefit plan, you had better start worrying about how the company is handling your retirement plan. Do it now before you are in your 50s and in trouble.

Understand how the terms in Chapter 9 relate to your company's compensation scheme. It is important that you understand not just how much you get, but why you get it, and which term explains it.

Part 6

COMPENSATION SYSTEMS

Chapter 10

BEST-OF-BOTH-WORLDS MODEL

In the past two chapters we examined the cultural framework of international compensation and reviewed some of the more common expatriate allowances. Using this discussion as a frame of reference we shall, in this chapter, first explore a set of principles and then view these principles within the context of a model system.

International Compensation Principles

The following compensation principles act as a background to the best-of-both-worlds model.

Everyone Has a Home Country Concept

In order to make intelligent decisions, it is necessary to anchor culturally derived compensation variables to a constant; this constant is the expatriate's home country. Relating compensation to a home country accomplishes the following: (a) establishes a structure against which the modular approach to expatriation allowances can be applied; (b) provides a cultural frame of reference in which to make compensation decisions; and (c) keeps the expatriate thinking of the home country compensation values, thus making repatriation less traumatic.

107

In most cases it is simple to define a home country. There are some circumstances, such as the expatriate who has married outside his home country or has transferred often over widely dispersed geographical and cultural areas, where this decision is more difficult. In these cases the country-of-retirement index is used. Where will the expatriate eventually retire? Once this is decided, the country of retirement becomes the home country for compensation purposes.

Modular Approach

The fundamentals of this approach are the following:

Philosophy of explanation—The company must be able to explain and the expatriate must be able to understand why allowances are paid, what hazards or differences they pay for, and how they are derived.

Pay only for differences—Expatriation allowances are developed to pay only for differences between host and home country.

No gain/no loss—Although it is impossible to guarantee that an expatriate will not gain or lose in terms of the home country compensation level, the philosophical intent of a modular approach is to keep the employee whole without allowing him to gain. Under this concept, the intent is that he break even. It is not intended that the expatriate make money relative to where he would have been if he had remained in his home country. Specific modules of his compensation package are, therefore, set up to expedite this philosophy. He is paid, for example, a cost-of-living allowance so that he remains whole in terms of his home country purchasing power. He is paid housing differentials and other allowances for the same "keep whole" reasons.

Under this concept, tax equalization becomes easier to understand. The expatriate assigned to a host country where it is possible to pay no taxes will still be asked to contribute a hypothetical tax. The no-gain/no-loss concept makes this just as philosophically acceptable as the expatriate who is assigned to a host country with a much larger income tax rate than his home country.

The no-gain/no-loss philosophy, like all principles, must be tempered with reality. As will be seen in the best-of-both-worlds model, there are circumstances where the no-loss half of the equation is all that is of concern. This does not mean no gain/no loss is not a valid concept, only that in the reality of international transfers, the no-loss half tends to receive more weight.

Taxation Characteristics

The principles of a tax system are the following:

It is honest—It does not attempt to play games with where and how salaries are paid in order to help the expatriate avoid income tax, or to avoid company tax equalization costs.

It uses tax minimization not tax avoidance schemes—Legal ways to minimize taxes are used, illegal ways to avoid taxes are not used.

It assumes responsibility for assuring that the expatriate complies with tax reporting laws—To this end, the company may provide an outside consultant to prepare and review the expatriate's tax return.

Uniform Classification Scheme

It is important that uniform people classification schemes exist across national borders. The salary range for an engineer in Country A may be substantially more than for an identical engineer in Country B. The important thing is that both countries have the concept of a salary range. The objective of a uniform classification scheme is that a company have the ability to equate salary, benefits, and tax levels among countries.

Elements of the Best-of-Both-Worlds Model

This model is offered as one example of a systems approach to expatriate compensation.

Element 1: Base Salary

Base salary, for purposes of this model, consists of that portion of compensation granted on a regular basis, exclusive of bonuses or other compensation. The model further makes the following assumptions: (a) *worldwide classification* (a uniform method of classifying and pricing jobs) and (b) *utilization of salary ranges* (a method of classification indicating the minimum, midpoint, and maximum salaries paid for any one job).

Types of Transfers

With the exception of a lateral transfer between two countries with identical salary levels (an almost impossible circumstance), there are the following two types of transfers: (a) An expatriate is transferred to a country with a lower base salary structure than his home country or (b) an expatriate is transferred to a country with a higher base salary structure than his home country.

Figure 1 indicates a transfer from a low-salary home country to a high-salary host country. For purposes of this model, it is assumed that the person makes a lateral transfer to a similar position in the host country. In this case the following happens:

- The expatriate is adjusted to a similar position in the host country salary range.

Figure 1

Salary Range Differential for Transfer From Low-Salary to High-Salary Country

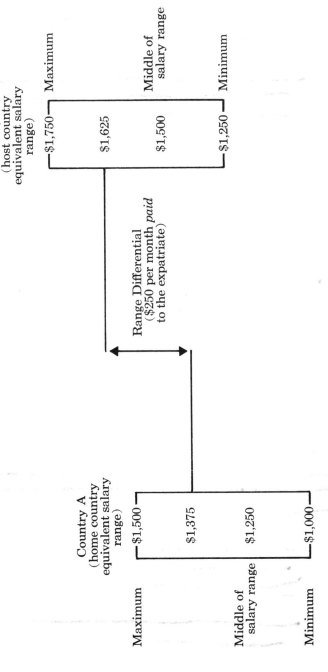

Note — Salaries are expressed in U.S. dollars per month. Subsequent salary reviews may affect the individual's position in his home country salary range while not necessarily affecting his salary in the host country.

- The monetary difference between these similar range positions is communicated to him as a range differential allowance.

- Any salary increases may not be reflected in his host country salary, but would certainly be shown in his home country salary. (In this way he retains any increases upon repatriation and his home country compensation is kept on par with other individuals in his home country.)

Figure 2 shows a transfer from a high-salary to a low-salary country. It is not realistic to expect an expatriate to take a base salary decrease for an overseas assignment, particularly in light of the no-gain/no-loss concept. Therefore, in this transaction the person transferring from Country A to Country B retains his home country salary. For administrative purposes he may be shown as occupying a similar position in the Country B salary structure. The difference may also be referred to as a range differential. Salary increases will be reflected in his home country salary when he returns. They may not be paid to him while on assignment.

Under this concept the expatriate receives the best of both worlds. If he transfers from a high-salary country to a low-salary country, he retains his home country base. If the reverse happens, he is adjusted to his host country salary. The advantages of this approach are as follows:

- It is unrealistic to expect expatriates under the no-gain/no-loss concept to take a salary decrease while transferring to a country where the base compensation is lower.

- In most cases, expatriates transferring from low-salary to high-salary countries would have a difficult

Figure 2

Salary Range Differential for Transfer From High-Salary to Low-Salary Country

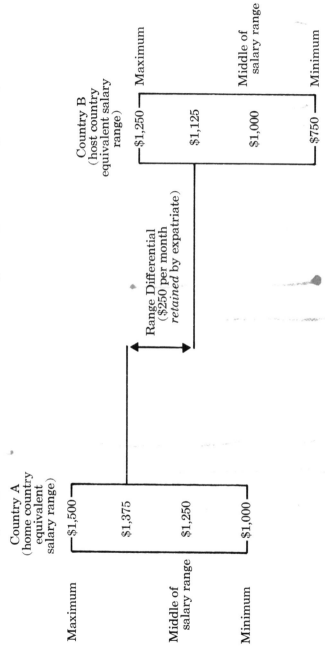

Note — Salaries are expressed in U.S. dollars per month. Subsequent salary increases will be reflected when the individual returns to the home country and may not necessarily be reflected in his salary when on assignment.

time existing if they were given only their home country salary. The salary range differential concept allows the expatriate to relate to his home country salary level while at the same time allows him to have the purchasing power of his host country peers.

- The model allows flexibility for recomputing salary range differentials on subsequent third-country transfers. In both cases (high salary to low salary and low salary to high salary), if an individual were to transfer to a third country, a new salary range differential would be computed based on his home country.

Salary Range Differential Relationship to Cost of Living

High-salary to low-salary transfer—Under this model a typical example of this situation is the transfer of an American to Belgium. The American will be allowed to take his U.S. salary to Brussels. In most cases, he will additionally be given a cost-of-living allowance. The rationale for this is that goods and services simply cost more in Brussels than in the United States and, utilizing the no-gain/no-loss concept, the lack of a cost-of-living allowance and a U.S. salary would cause the expatriate to lose.

Low-salary to high-salary transfers—An example of this type of transfer would be the reverse, i.e., a Belgian transferring to the United States. He would, no doubt, receive a salary range differential when transferred to the U.S. scale. The salary range differential in this case could also be referred to as a cost-of-living allowance. The assumption is that the U.S. salary range includes an offset amount for the difference in purchasing power.

The American sent to Brussels would not only be allowed to keep his U.S. salary but also be granted a cost-of-living allowance to buy goods and services as though he were in America. However, the Belgian, while adjusted to the U.S.

salary structure, would not be granted an additional cost-of-living allowance.

There is a case for granting the Belgian a cost-of-living allowance if a survey could be found that measured the cost of Belgian culturally derived goods and services in the United States and proved that these items were both available and more expensive. In the majority of circumstances this type of information is just not available in reliable form. Usually the expatriate who is transferred from a low- to a high-salary country must be content with the range differential allowance.

Element 2: Taxes

The second element of the best-of-both-worlds model deals with income tax levels. Again there are two possibilities: transferring from a low-tax country to a high-tax country or the reverse.

Figure 3 depicts a transfer from a low-tax country to a high-tax country. In this case the expatriate is tax equalized to his host (low-tax) country. He, in essence, pays his company a "hypothetical" tax. The company then assumes his host country tax burden. The expatriate's hypothetical tax is based on what he would have paid if he had remained in his home country. (Another example of the no-gain/no-loss situation.) If, by virtue of living outside his home country, he is not liable for home country taxes, he still pays his hypothetical tax to his company. This is part of the balance sheet (everyone must pay a tax somewhere) approach and can be related back to the no-gain portion of the no-gain/no-loss equation.

Figure 4 depicts an expatriate transferring from a high-tax to a low-tax country. In this case, under the best-of-both-worlds model, the expatriate pays the host country tax rate. The company assumes any remaining or duplicate home country taxes once the expatriate leaves. Under this model,

Figure 3

Tax Differential for Transfer From Low-Tax to High-Tax Country

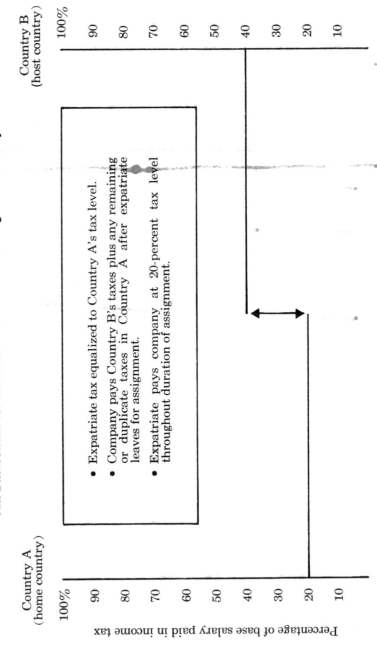

- Expatriate tax equalized to Country A's tax level.
- Company pays Country B's taxes plus any remaining or duplicate taxes in Country A after expatriate leaves for assignment.
- Expatriate pays company at 20-percent tax level throughout duration of assignment.

Country A (home country)

100%
90
80
70
60
50
40
30
20
10

Percentage of base salary paid in income tax

Country B (host country)

100%
90
80
70
60
50
40
30
20
10

Figure 4

Tax Differential for Transfer From High-Tax to Low-Tax Country

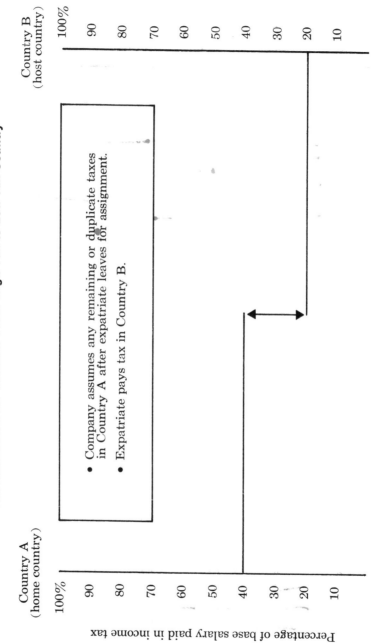

• Company assumes any remaining or duplicate taxes in Country A after expatriate leaves for assignment.

• Expatriate pays tax in Country B.

Country A (home country)

Country B (host country)

Percentage of base salary paid in income tax

expatriates who are transferred from low-tax to high-tax countries are tax equalized to their home country rates. Expatriates who are transferred from high- to low-tax countries are tax protected to their host country rates. This treatment has the following advantages:

- Expatriates transferring from a low- to high-tax country are related back to their home country and suffer no adverse tax effects.

- Expatriates transferring from high- to low-tax situations are able to derive more net income by paying the lower (host country) tax. Since many low-tax countries are also high-salary countries, the idea of the salary range adjustment as a cost-of-living allowance becomes more understandable.

In the case of the Belgian (low salary, high tax) transferring to the United States (high salary, low tax) the adjustment to the higher salary and the lower tax would provide a net income increase that could be easily explained as a cost-of-living adjustment instead of a range differential allowance.

The best-of-both-worlds tax model utilizes elements of both tax protection and tax equalization. Table 2 indicates three tax philosophies.

Element 3: Benefits

The third element in the best-of-both-worlds model is that of benefits. Figure 5 indicates the treatment of benefits with the following components:

- The home country has a 5-percent contributory retirement plan. The host country has none. The expatriate is continued in the home country plan during his entire expatriation assignment.

Table 2

Three Types of Tax Philosophies

Type I (laissez-faire)	Type II (tax protection)	Type III (tax equalization)
• Expatriate fends for himself. • Company is not concerned with expatriate's tax obligations. • Expatriate is free to choose to pay or evade home or host country tax obligations.	• Company guarantees expatriate no more tax obligation than he would have incurred in the home country. • Company helps expatriate avoid tax liabilities by splitting income. • Company is not concerned if expatriate can avoid taxes in host or home country; only concerned to the extent of exercising guarantee of no more taxes.	• Company controls tax payment, i.e., guarantees no more than he would have paid if he had stayed in the home country. • Company is legal in reporting taxes; utilizes tax minimization schemes but reports worldwide income. • Company utilizes outside consultant to assure consistency of tax submissions. • Expatriate pays hypothetical tax to company, even if on tax-free assignment.

Figure 5

Best-of-Both-Worlds Benefits Model

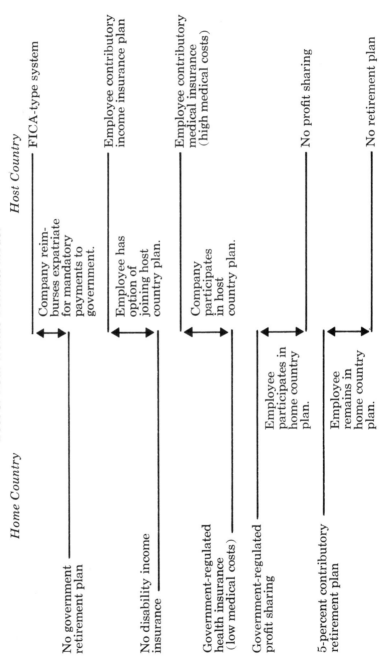

- The home country also has a government-regulated profit-sharing plan in which the company must set aside a percentage of its profits for pay out on an annual basis to the employee. There is no profit sharing in the host country. Once again, relating back to home country and the no-gain/no-loss concept, the expatriate is maintained in the home country profit-sharing program, and an amount is set aside as though he were in that country.

- In the area of health insurance there is no private plan in the expatriate's home country benefit package. This is due to the fact that medical costs are low and regulated by the government; however, in his host country medical costs are high, not regulated by the government, and a private insurance plan is the norm. In this case the expatriate participates in the host country medical insurance plan. Strict interpretation of the no-gain/no-loss concept would dictate that the expatriate pay no higher premiums for equivalent medical coverage than he would have paid if he had remained in his home country. Such a calculation, however, becomes administratively difficult, and, in most cases, expatriates simply pay the same premiums as other host country employees.

- In the area of disability income insurance, there is no plan in the home country; there is, however, a plan in the host country. In this case, also, the expatriate has the option, as do other host country employees, to participate in the plan.

- In the area of government retirement plans, the home country has no plan; however, the host country does and requires mandatory withholding of premiums. Because the expatriate will retire to his home country, he should not become involved in host country retirement plans. In this case the host country receives the mandatory source withholding, and the expatriate is reimbursed by his company for the amount withheld.

If this transaction were reversed, the following would happen:

- The expatriate would participate in his home country FICA-type system and not in the host country privately funded retirement plan.

- He would have the option of remaining in his home country disability income insurance program.

- He would have the option of remaining in his home country medical insurance plan; however, he may choose to drop the plan while overseas if the host country has a better cost:benefit ratio with its government-supported program. Expatriates exercising this option, however, must be sure that they can get back into their home country plan upon return. Many have physical examination requirements, and the expatriate may be better off paying into the plan during his overseas assignment rather than risking loss of reinstatement upon repatriation.

- Conceptually, the expatriate would be allowed to participate in the host country profit sharing. There may even be a legal requirement for him to receive profit-sharing monies, since the government could require payment to all employees. Since the expatriate is working for the host country organization, the company may legally have no choice. However, expatriates receiving culturally derived profit-sharing plans in their host country tend not only to irritate local employees but also to violate the no-gain/no-loss principle, particularly if these profit-sharing plans relate to a percentage of base pay and the base pay of the expatriate is derived from a home country salary range which is higher than the host country range. To solve this problem, some multinationals have requested that their employees refuse these payments and if granted by the government, place them into a general fund for national employees.

Individualized Tailoring

The principles and model described in this chapter offer one method of dealing with compensation-related issues. Each multinational employer needs to develop an individual system to relate to its unique problems. The best-of-both-worlds model can, however, serve as a frame of reference when structuring individual company systems.

A system is only as good as its implementation. In order to implement a system, such as the best-of-both-worlds model, a delivery and control system is needed. This is the subject of the next chapter.

Chapter 11

DELIVERY AND CONTROL

Paper Tiger

A U.S.-based multinational decided it needed a compensation system for its rapidly growing expatriate population. A task force was formed, consultants were retained, and six months later a very sophisticated expatriate compensation system was born.

The birth was easy; the growth pains were hard. The system was less than a year old when the company discovered not only that all the good things in its new policy were not happening but also that it was in serious trouble with the taxing authorities in some countries. The company found that it needed more than paper to hold its system together. The company needed a delivery and control system to make certain that its new policy was implemented.

The internal audit department was the first to point out that the new system only served as stuffing to the corporate policy manual; the problems were still the same. A management review revealed the following:

- In some cases expatriate expenses (salaries and allowances) were claimed as a cost of doing business in both the home and host country; in others, expenses were claimed in the wrong country (not the one where services were performed); while in still

124

other cases, the company was not claiming its expenses on either side of the ocean.

- The expatriates had no confidence in the accuracy of their paychecks. Some were paid too much, others went through pay periods without anything, and a number simply refused to accept their check, living instead on a series of advances until someone from management could explain what went into their pay calculations. Regardless of whether they were paid too much or too little, all were experiencing a loss in confidence in the company—a serious matter when added to the other complications of expatriate life.

- All allowances were lumped together, even though some were taxable to the expatriates and others were paid by the company. The employees had nightmares of attempting to communicate with the company-retained tax consultants in order to prepare their personal income tax returns.

- Benefit deductions were totally snarled. The company had a policy *similar* to the best-of-both-worlds model which required a method of keeping track of deductions on both ends of the assignment, but they did not have this capability; the result was administrative chaos with the expatriate having no idea what was deducted where.

- Host country payroll functions were confused, and managers were wasting too much time on both sides of the assignment attempting to untangle the situation.

This example illustrates the basic fact that a company may have the best policies and procedures in existence, but without a delivery and control system they become just so much paper. It is necessary to structure and institutionalize the mechanical aspects of something as geographically dispersed and as complex as an expatriate compensation system.

Expatriate Payroll and Tax Model

One example of an effective delivery and control system is the expatriate payroll and tax model. It has the following characteristics:

- Centralized expatriate payroll administration—All expatriate salaries are administered by one central source. This centralized expatriate payroll function is responsible for assuring prompt and accurate payment of expatriate premiums and salaries. All expatriates are paid in local currency units on a month-lag basis. The centralized payroll function uses a turnaround document authorizing local country paymasters to pay expatriates. No expatriate is paid without a specific authorization each month. If any items, such as educational allowances or storage charges, are paid in the host country, the expenses are reported to the centralized payroll and tax function for inclusion in computing the expatriate's gross income and also for claiming tax credits on the company's tax return.

- Tax monitoring, calculation of tax equalization amounts, reporting of taxable income to both host and home country, and administration of individual income tax returns—These are all coordinated by this function.

- Centralized control—A centralized system acts as a control mechanism. No one can be expatriated without proper approval because he will not be paid; only approved transactions go through the system. Any changes in allowances that result in changing the expatriate's net income are also handled through the system.

Donald's Departure

In order to gain an insider's view of the workings of the expatriate payroll and tax model, we will follow an expatriate through the system. Donald and his family will be expatriated from the United States to New Zealand for three years. Let us look over their shoulders.

Cost Estimate

Before Donald was even selected, a cost estimate was prepared by the expatriate payroll and tax function. This indicated how much it would cost in base salary, expatriation premiums, tax equalization, relocation, and home leave expenses to keep Donald and his family overseas. This is the first stage of any control system. In many cases, midnight decisions to send people on expatriate assignments have been reversed when, in the cold light of reality, the manager sees the total costs of his decision.

Tax Equalization Session

Donald and his spouse determine, with someone from the expatriate payroll and tax function, the amount of money they would have paid in income tax if they had remained in the United States. There are a number of methods to arrive at this figure. Donald's company, processing a large number and utilizing a standard calculation, used the 3 by 5 method. In this equation, the percentage of Donald's gross income paid in state and federal income taxes was computed for each of the past five years. The high and low were thrown out and the remaining three years were averaged. The resulting percentage was applied to Donald's taxable income and deducted from his pay. (Upon his return, the amount of deduction was audited and adjusted based on variables such as salary increases or outside income.)

Salary Calculation

Donald's monthly salary was calculated by taking his base salary, subtracting his tax equalization contribution or hypothetical tax, and adding his expatriation allowances. (They are tax free in this model.) The result was a total number of U.S. dollars to be paid to Donald. This amount was then converted to New Zealand currency, using the exchange rate in existence at the time.

Move Overseas

Donald and his family flew to New Zealand. His salary was paid on a month-lag basis. It was based on a form sent by the centralized expatriate payroll and tax function to the paymaster in Wellington. In Donald's case, this transaction was as follows: (a) Donald chose to have 25 percent of his income paid into a bank in the United States. (b) The payroll and tax system accommodated this by sending 25 percent of his income to the U.S. bank and instructing the paymaster in Wellington to pay only 75 percent. (Since Donald was paid on a month-lag basis, he could change this whenever he desired by simply writing to the proper person in the payroll and tax function. It is possible for an expatriate, under this system, to change the percentage of his pay brought into the host country each month if that is his desire.) (c) This was not, however, splitting his income to avoid taxes because his total salary and allowances were reported to New Zealand and the United States. Part of his monthly income was simply paid in the United States as a convenience to Donald, not as a way of hiding it.

Host Country Allowances

The system responds to the need to report locally paid allowances to the home country. Donald sent his children to a private school in Wellington. Under the company's educational allowance policy, this was paid by the company. When the monthly payroll authorization form was sent to New Zealand indicating the amount of money Donald had due, the paymaster paid the amount indicated, entered the amount of tuition paid locally on the turnaround section of the form, and sent it back to the payroll and tax function.

Outside Tax Consultant

At the end of the year Donald had two tax obligations. One was the portion of time he spent in the United States; the other was the time he spent in New Zealand. The model assumes that the company pays for an outside tax consultant (one who does business throughout the world) to do individual tax returns. Donald was put in contact with the local branch of the tax consultant, who prepared his tax returns for both host and home countries. Since New Zealand's tax rates were higher than the U.S. rates for Donald, he was put on tax equalization (the best-of-both-worlds model), and the New Zealand taxes were paid by his company.

Devaluation/Revaluation

During Donald's second year, the U.S. dollar devalued. This meant that it took more U.S. dollars to buy New Zealand dollars. If Donald were paid in U.S. dollars (a dollar check sent to him each month), he would be concerned because he would essentially be taking a pay cut equal to the amount of the devaluation; however, Donald's pay was given to him in New Zealand dollars. (Also, the 25 percent of his salary that he left in the United States remained unchanged.)

Table 3 illustrates Donald's situation if we assume that the total amount of money (base plus allowances) Donald wished shipped to New Zealand the month prior to the devaluation was $1,000 U.S. currency and that $1,000 U.S.

currency bought $880 New Zealand dollars prior to the devaluation and $800 after devaluation.

Table 3

Currency Valuation Allowance

	U.S. dollars	New Zealand dollars
Prior to devaluation	$1,000	$880
After devaluation	$1,000	$800
Amount of U.S. dollars needed to give Donald the same New Zealand dollars received before devaluation	$1,100	$880
When Donald returns to United States (assuming no salary increases or further currency valuation changes)	$1,000*	—

*He does not receive the extra $100 (currency valuation allowance) because the calculation was made to keep him whole in terms of his host country income while on assignment.

It can be seen that in order to guarantee Donald the same net income he had the previous month, a currency valuation allowance was necessary. This will be a permanent allowance for as long as the currency relationship remains stable or until Donald repatriates. There are two reasons for an allowance rather than simply guaranteeing Donald the same New Zealand dollars as before devaluation. First, the company must account for differences in the cost of money. Second, the payroll and tax model is dynamic. Donald can change the amount he wishes to bring into New Zealand.

What happens, for example, if he wishes to purchase a car the month *after* devaluation and brings in 100 percent of his salary? Does he receive the predevaluation exchange rate? No, not under the model. The assumption is made that he is protected by the host country net income based on the net he was paid the month prior to the devaluation. What this assumption lacks in flexibility, it gains in administrative workability.

There was a possibility that Donald could have made some money in currency speculation by anticipating the devaluation and electing to ship more money into the host country the month before it happened. While discouraging currency speculation on the part of its expatriates, Donald's company is concerned with the equitable administration of a system rather than with the possibility of a few expatriates speculating in currency relationships.

What happens during a revaluation of currency in the home country? The opposite of what happened to Donald. The currency valuation adder becomes negative as shown in Number 2 in Table 4.

Cost of Living

Cost-of-living computations are also affected by currency fluctuations. Most market basket studies use the U.S. dollar to buy local currency units to purchase goods and services. When the cost of these units rises or falls, the cost-of-living allowance must also be adjusted. Assuming Donald received a cost-of-living allowance in New Zealand, it would not change. He is already protected with a currency valuation allowance that related back to his past month's host country net which, of course, included his cost-of-living allowance. However, the new cost-of-living allowance would apply to a U.S. expatriate who arrived in New Zealand after the devaluation, because this person would not have a currency valuation allowance and would transfer under the new (lower) exchange rates.

Table 4

Devaluation/Revaluation Expressed in U.S. Dollar Relationship To Local Currency Units

	U.S. dollars	Local currency units

1. Devaluation (The number of U.S. dollars needed to buy local currency units increases.)

	U.S. dollars	Local currency units
Predevaluation	1	5
Postdevaluation*	1	4

2. Revaluation (The number of U.S. dollars needed to buy local currency units decreases.)

	U.S. dollars	Local currency units
Predevaluation	1	5
Postdevaluation†	1	6

Note—In the case of non-U.S. to non-U.S. currency changes, substitute the home country currency units where U.S. dollars are indicated.

*Under this situation, it would take $1.25 U.S. dollars to purchase the same 5 local currency units. Therefore, a currency valuation allowance would be computed.

†Under this situation, it would take approximately $.83 U.S. dollars to purchase the same local currency units. Therefore, the currency valuation allowance would be a negative value.

Floats

What would happen to Donald if there were no formal devaluation, but the U.S. dollar were allowed to float downward against the New Zealand dollar? The system must accommodate floats; they are more common than formal changes in currency relationships. The method of responding to floats is the setting of percentage parameters, beyond which currency valuation allowances are computed. In Donald's company, currency valuation allowances are computed if the exchange rate varies more than 3 percent for over 90 days from the rate at the time of his initial expatriation.

Terminology Revisited

Before closing this chapter, it is necessary to review briefly the use of the common expatriate allowances in light of the principles and models discussed.

Expatriation premium—When viewed within the conceptual framework of a modular no-gain/no-loss system, expatriation premiums granted without relation to a specific problem do not appear to make sense.

Cost-of-living allowance—The best-of-both-worlds model suggests that the administrative problems and lack of valid data inherent in attempting to apply a cost-of-living index to most transfers from a low-salary country to a high-salary country can be alleviated by simply calling the salary range differential a cost-of-living allowance.

Many U.S. multinationals are beginning to question the long-term necessity of paying the cost-of-living allowances. Some are attempting to relate learning curves to cost-of-living allowances. Under this concept, a cost-of-living allowance would mean more the first year of an assignment. The assumption is made that the expatriate family would learn how to shop and would be able to purchase goods and services in a more efficient and less expensive manner the longer they live in a country.

This concept also responds to the experience of many multinational managers that the expatriate family begins to value its culturally derived standards less the longer it is in a foreign location. The family begins to go national in terms of its purchasing preferences and, thus, does not have the same need for a cost-of-living allowance as the newly arrived expatriate family.

Declining premiums also tend to have the effect of forcing some expatriates to think of returning home. This helps those companies with the problem of expatriates staying on assignments too long. If the longer they stay, the smaller their cost-of-living allowance, there may be a tendency for them to accelerate finishing the job and returning home. Table 5 shows a declining cost-of-living table.

Table 5

Declining Cost-of-Living Table

Year	% paid per month	Dollar amount
1	150	600
2	100	400
3	50	200
4	25	100
5	0	0

Note—Assumption: cost-of-living index is 40 percent of host country base of $1,000 per month.

Swamp pay—The utilization of all forms of swamp pay is diminishing. Its use should be limited to countries of demonstrable hazards, and then reviewed regularly for appropriateness.

Housing allowance—The best-of-both-worlds model allows the expatriate whose home country has large U.S.-style housing to secure this type of accommodation while overseas. At the same time, the expatriate coming from a country with small housing units would not be limited to such units if larger units were generally available.

There is a trend toward rental protection on home country housing. Many companies are recommending that the expatriate consider renting, rather than selling, his home and are assisting both with maintenance and protection against his house payments in case the house is without a renter. The reasons for this trend toward rental protection are as follows: (a) Rental protection can be less expensive to the company than paying a real estate fee. (b) With the increased cost of housing, lack of money to borrow, and high-interest rates, some returned expatriates have been unable to purchase homes upon their return. Some have been unable to purchase homes equivalent to those they sold before leaving. (c) Owning property in a home country is another way of relating an expatriate to his country. This is philosophically desirable in most companies.

Total System

This chapter has shown an example of a delivery and control system which, when combined with the best-of-both-worlds model, results in a total systems approach to expatriation. The total systems approach dictates not only sophisticated compensation policies but also a delivery and control system to support them.

TO THE EXPATRIATE

It is not necessary to have an in-depth knowledge of your company's compensation system, but you had better find out if your company has one at all. The issues covered by the best-of-both-worlds model provide a checklist. How does your company handle the problems of salary, benefits, and tax relationships across borders? How do you know if your company does the same for each expatriate? What is your company's system?

If the system responds to the problems handled by the best-of-both-worlds model, how do you know your company will be able to deliver the goods? Is the system only on paper, or does it really work? In short, what kind of delivery and control system does your company use?

It is important to understand the basics of your system before moving overseas. Things are complicated enough over there. Do not add to the confusion by not understanding the method your pay is computed, transferred, or converted into local currency rates. Find out what happens when currency relationships change before you move rather than spending your overseas time attempting to unsnarl conversion rates.

Take the trip to New Zealand again, only this time put yourself and your company in the picture. Trace through the way Donald's delivery and control system handled his move. How will your company handle your situation?

136

Take time before you go to discuss your company's system with your boss, and your personnel manager if you have one. If they do not understand your questions, do two things: give them a copy of this book and work hard to structure your assignment so that at least the company will have one expatriate who has taken a systems approach to moving overseas.

Part 7

THE FUTURE

Chapter 12

BRIDGE BUILDERS

It is apparent to all but those holding the most unshakable isolationist philosophy that mankind shares a world of economic interdependence. Solutions to problems, such as unemployment and inflation, must be made on a worldwide scale. Nothing else will work in a world forced to share energy and technology resources.

While the forces of survival are driving toward worldwide management of energy and technology, the power of nationalism and culture is pushing people inward. The need for economic ecumenicalism is not eradicating cultural and nationalistic differences, if anything it is clearing the air, removing the mists from the chasms of nationalism, and sharpening our perception as to their true depth.

The future will dictate a global allocation of resources, yet at the same time it will demand a response toward cultural and nationalistic desires. What institution will respond to the dilemma? Who will build tomorrow's bridges over the nationalistic chasms that separate our world? The bridges may be designed by governments, but the prime contractors will be the multinational companies. They have the knowledge and experience.

The short-range future of the multinational enterprise may, at times of isolationist response to economic ills, seem dim. The long-range potential, however, is outstanding. The multinational company will be the prime contractor for our future survival. It has experience in responding to the push of nationalism and the pull of the survival need for worldwide planning. It can respond to the dilemma. It has experience in the schizophrenic problems of balancing nationalistic desires and worldwide answers.

What are the implications of tomorrow's role of the multinational company to the expatriate? There appear to be two: (a) The key ingredient for better multinational decisions will be cross-cultural experience. There will, therefore, be a continuing need for people with more than one-country experience. This experience may well be a prerequisite for advancement into top management in tomorrow's multinational. (b) Tomorrow's expatriate will be much more sophisticated. Tomorrow's expatriate will view today's in the same manner we look at the pith-helmeted colonialist of yesterday. The effective expatriate of the future will need the skills to bridge the chasms of nationalism. He will be able to live in the deepest cultural valley, yet have the skills necessary to scale the cliffs and make worldwide decisions.

The Future Environment

Tomorrow's expatriate will not have an easy environment in which to ply his trade. He will exist in an atmosphere of distrust. The multinational company will be involved in the implementation of decisions for everyone, and therefore will please no one. The expatriate of the future must be prepared to respond to issues ranging from job exportation in large countries to fear of dominance in small countries.

There will be a decline of headquarters country bias. Decisions that are biased toward headquarters countries will not be tolerated in tomorrow's world. People decisions will not be tainted by the home country of the person. Just as technology and energy decisions will be made on a more-than-one-country basis, so will decisions on the allocation and utilization of human resources.

There will be a blurring of the differentiation between exploiter and exploitee. Countries such as the United States will take their places in the world labor market. Foreign ownership of plants and services in the United States will increase, just as the United States will continue to invest overseas.

Skills for Tomorrow

The multinational firm will need a far more sophisticated expatriate in the future. The basic framework for the development of these skills is outlined in this book.

The need for a philosophy is paramount. It will need to be related to the increasing local ownership, the thrust toward participative management, and the leveling of the roles of the exploiter/exploitee.

Selection will continue to be important. The future expatriate will need to have the bridge-building ability to cross nationalistic valleys, as well as the ability to relate to a specific culture. His compensation must also be culturally related. It must be packaged in a system he can understand and backed with a delivery and control system that works.

We are, all of us, contained in one planet. To a large degree our survival is dependent on worldwide decisions on technology, energy, and ecology. If the multinational enterprise is to be the prime contractor in the building of worldwide decision-making bridges across the chasms of nationalism, the individual expatriate is the worker. As such, he is a resource we can ill afford to underutilize, for he wields the pick and shovel of our future.

TO THE MULTINATIONAL EMPLOYER: A CHECKLIST

Today the multinational enterprise exists in an environment of misunderstanding and distrust. The future will not be easy; the demands will be harsh and the skills necessary to make worldwide decisions will be difficult to attain. The world is changing; energy is shrinking, communications are expanding, technology is becoming equally divided, and nationalism is sharpening. Development of the management skills necessary to steer an even path through tomorrow's world falls squarely upon the shoulders of the multinational employer. There is nowhere this development can take place more effectively than in an expatriate assignment. Unfortunately expatriate experiences tend to be binary; a bad experience can taint a potential worldwide decision maker beyond repair and that is why it is incumbent upon the multinational employer to do all that is possible to assure positive expatriate experiences. This book has explored a basic framework for the management of the multinational employee. The purpose of the following checklist is to enable the multinational employer to relate this framework to his individual circumstances:

Philosophy

- Is there a written expatriate philosophy? Is it understood and used?
- Are transfers between countries and within one country handled differently?
- Is there an effort to define the reasons for sending a person overseas? How does the rationale relate to the valid and invalid reasons on pages 21 and 22?

145

- Is the philosophy consistent with the organizational structure?
- Does the philosophy give a fall-back position in case of problems? How does your philosophy operate in the case of Teddy (page 23)? Would it help with Trevor's problem (page 25)?
- Are definitions well understood? Does everyone understand what an expatriate is?
- Is your philosophy consistent with the evolving trends outlined on page 28?
- Does your company relate the expatriate to his home country? What happens when he returns? Does your company have a system that accomplishes the objectives of the godfather system?

Selection

- Are expatriates selected only on home country performance or are there other criteria?
- Do your expatriates view themselves as entrepreneurs or hirelings?
- Are off-the-job behavioral patterns considered in the selection process?
- Do the individuals making selection decisions understand their cultural bias and attempt to balance it with other opinions?
- Do those making selection decisions understand the country of assignment? Have they ever been there?
- Is the spouse involved in the selection process? Would your system have discovered the problem with Maynard's wife (page 51)?
- Is the selection process institutionalized? Is it consistent?

Orientation and Training

- Does your company have an expatriate orientation and training program? Are the barriers on page 64 found in your company?
- Are the terms and conditions of assignment reviewed with each candidate? Is a letter of understanding or a similar document used?
- Have there been cases of "our-company syndrome" as outlined on page 66 in your organization?

- Does your company become involved in any form of cultural training?
- Is language training a condition of assignment? Are expatriates given enough lead time to benefit from it? How often are the negative rationales listed on page 71 used?
- How does your orientation and training program measure up to that given Orville in Chapter 7?
- Does your company give a reentry orientation?

Compensation

- To what degree does your company export home country compensation values? Have you had any situations similar to that of the Asian administrator on page 88?
- Does your expatriate compensation system account for cultural differences in the relationship among salary, benefits, and taxes?
- Is your system consistent? Has your company had the type of problem illustrated by the three men in Paris on page 90?
- Does your company allow expatriates to take advantage of local benefits as illustrated in the case of the "company car that broke the camel's back" on page 92?
- Does your system allow the career expatriate to have a retirement plan?
- Are the reasons for expatriate allowances clearly understood? Do these allowances complement your philosophy?
- Does your company have an overall expatriate compensation system? Does it meet the criteria outlined in the best-of-both-worlds model (Chapter 10)?
- Is your method of handling expatriate income taxes legal?
- Do you have a delivery and control system that works? How does it handle split pay, salary increases, currency valuation changes, and tax-reporting requirements?

Management Development

- Is your company using people with expatriate experience to help make more-than-one-country decisions?
- Do candidates for top management positions need to have expatriate experience?
- Are top managers trained to shed cultural bias in order to make worldwide decisions?

INDEX